Book edited and proofread by Alison Skinner | Proofreading

Also by this author…

The Great Glen Way
and
On Arran

Paul Brown

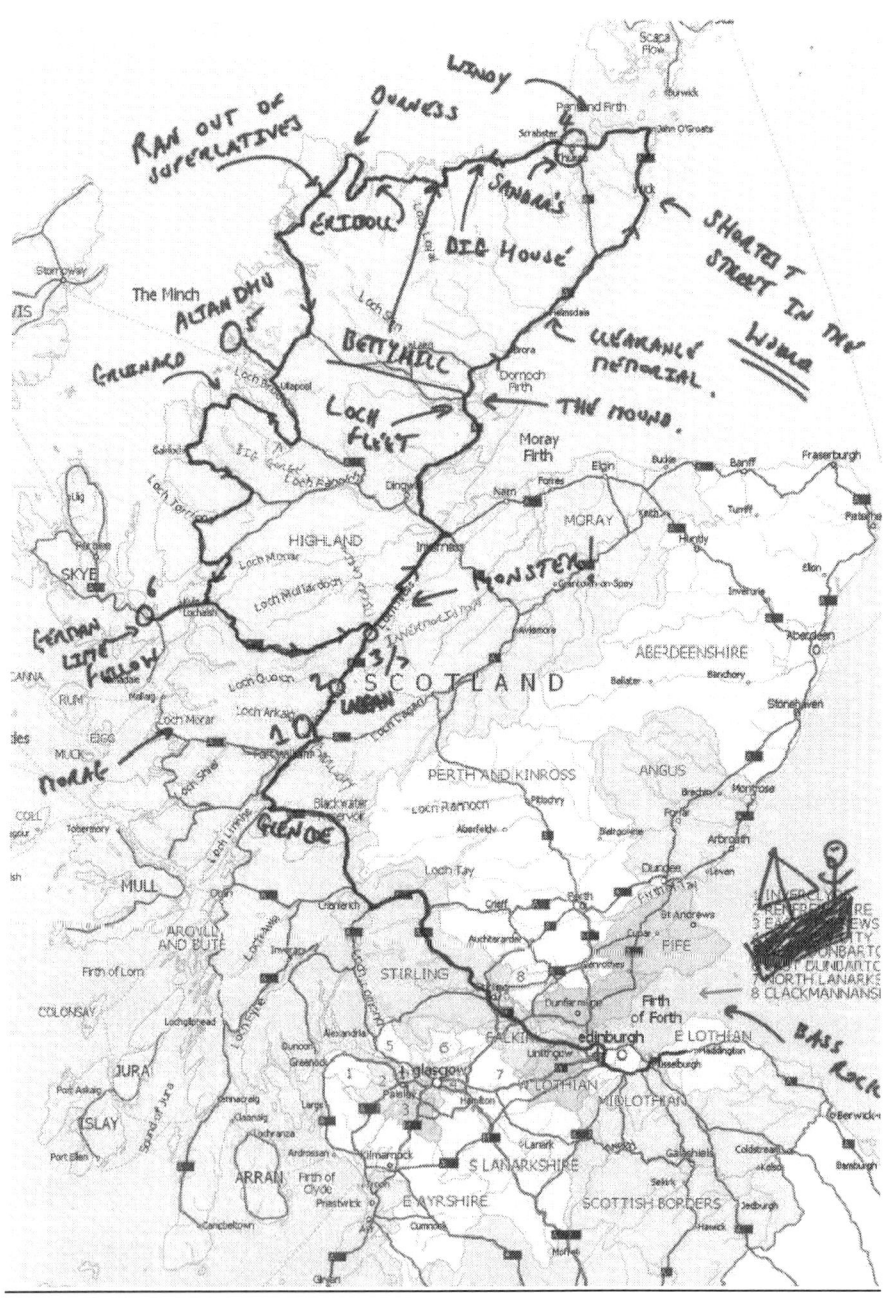

Contains OS data © Crown copyright and database right 2017

Base map © maproom.net

Contents

Foreword

It's traditional to have a foreword written by someone mildly famous or by a person with a link (however tenuous) to the thing your book is about. I don't really know anyone famous. I also couldn't think of anyone with links to the subject matter of this book to whom I could turn for wise and pertinent words. I mean, being a Scout leader I could have asked Bear Grylls and I dare say he would have wished me well, perhaps in a tweet, but I don't think he'd have furnished me with a foreword.

A friend who kindly read over an earlier draft of this book suggested I might like to add a prologue of sorts so readers had some context for the waffle it contained. It's also a good opportunity to manage some expectations; I mean I'm quite proud of what I've produced here – I think it's quite good. But I also understand that my perceptions (and personal bar) may be set at a different level to yours. So let me start by saying I'm writing this foreword last. It's been three years since the trip detailed here took place, and it's taken that long to get to this point.

If you cast your mind back to when you were in school – primary school, in particular – can you ever remember considering what your teacher did when they weren't showing you how to do long division or sending you along the corridor to the nit nurse? I didn't. I just assumed they went to the stationery cupboard and recharged in some esoteric and unknowable way. I think a lot of my current Scouts think the same way about me. Suffice to say, we leaders all have lives outside Scouts. Young people might catch us in the local shop buying vodka, or they might see us on the train coming home from work, or perhaps from a counselling session, say. During the writing of this, I moved three times, and bought and sold three motorcycles and more cars than I care to remember – each one more crap than the one it preceded.

I also placed one parent in a care home and another in the ground. Well, not in the ground, but it sounds good and works well as a narrative device – it was actually a cremation. My Dad died the week before Christmas 2015, and it is to him this book (such as it is) is dedicated. He retired from the world of work in April of 2008, but by the middle of May he was flat on his back in hospital suffering from chronic liver failure. I remember getting the phone call and making my way in to see him. I found the ward easily enough, but had to ask a nearby nurse if it was indeed him in the bed – he was a dull shade of yellow and diminished in so many respects that my own ability to recognise him suffered a failure of its own. My Dad quite enjoyed a whisky – Famous Grouse was his brand. He also enjoyed a good time, a really good time. Both of those things turned out to be his undoing. He managed to recover and live on for another six years or so, going from one medical emergency to the next. It turns out you don't just get chronic liver failure; family are introduced to a panoply of complications ranging from confusion, kidney dysfunction and chronic fluid retention through to Cardio

Pulmonary Obstructive Disorder, along with the dizzying menu of medications to treat and assuage it all with. That accounts for about half of it because family also embark upon an odyssey of discovery into social services, the NHS, occupational therapy, HM Revenues and Customs, and the Department for Work and Pensions. Things you've never heard of such as attendance allowance crop up, and strangers appear to make sure you're getting all the help you need – so much so that you need help dealing with all the different people who turn up to help.

Of course, it wasn't all bad. We all got an extra six years or so with him, and while they were challenging in places, in others they were memorable for other reasons. A couple of years into his career with liver failure, he also went deaf. Due to the encephalopathy (a big word that means confusion), it meant he didn't have the presence of mind to understand that while he couldn't hear himself, others still could. Boy could he shout. When you couple that with a pre-existing tendency toward a smutty sense of humour (enhanced to a bionic level by the encephalopathy), you fast learn what it means to cringe from the soles of your feet to the tips of your ears. Of course, he had no idea he was doing anything wrong. It's one thing to pass comment on the proportions another person's, ummm, person – it's quite another to do so at a rate of decibels that guarantees the person (usually a female nurse) being talked about hears it, along with all of her colleagues, other patients, doctors, consultants, registrars and the people working in the hospital canteen two floors down. Fortunately, he had a certain charm and was well known by hospital staff – he also had an impressive Magnum PI-style moustache, which I like to think helped.

When he eventually died, we'd lost count of the number of emergency hospital admissions he'd had. You can only remain at a certain level of readiness for so long – certainly, being on tenterhooks for six years is not supportable. It was simultaneously a surprise and not a surprise when eventually he did shuffle off. We had his funeral on Hogmanay, which I thought was apt given how much he liked to party. We all had a drink – make of that what you will – to his memory and as much as any death can feel okay, his sort of did.

We also had to move my Mum into a care home during that time. She's still with us – battling on with Parkinson's disease and Dementia with Lewy Bodies. I wish I could explain what the latter thing was. I read up on it some time ago, but it's easier to say it has most of the symptoms of dementia, but with a slightly different cause (Lewy Bodies). Having already been through it with my Dad, having to step in again for Mum was less of a shock.

On balance, I'd prefer it if they'd both had healthy retirements spent walking in the local countryside, on cruises or with friends. But what can you do?

I now feel as if I'm going on about things, you should know, the book you bought is indeed a mildly diverting, informative and humorous travelogue, not a tale of woe or plea for pity. I didn't write it to garner sympathy from readers, I wrote it because Scotland is a great place to visit and travel around and doing it with young people in tow makes it fresh and fun in a way going with other adults wouldn't be. Even in this day of Google Maps, webcams and mass transport, there are parts of this small country that are still well off the beaten track and rarely if ever visited. Sadly as these areas become more accessible – or as the great roiling masses (that would be me and you), realise they're not as out of reach as we think they are - these hitherto quiet, unvisited places, will become ever busier. So, if you're going to go, you should go now. I know that statement is self-defeating because you will be part of the growing crowds visiting, but that's progress and you may-as-well get in early. I hope the far north and west of Scotland never loses its unspoiled charm, but I worry that it might end up more like the Great Glen and less like the great wilderness it should always be.

This foreword, in places, might seem like a particularly long excuse for not doing my homework, but it should be noted that I also work. Although I use that term loosely – I'm supposed to be working now, but I'm doing this instead. I wish I could tell the young folk in Scouts tales of daring élan at my place of work, but it's all rather boring. I work for the NHS, and when I have work to do, it's usually to do with changing room lockers, racking or bins. There are other things we do too: I sit beside people that know all about super-expensive, hi-tech imaging and monitoring equipment. Medical professionals might know how to operate these things, but they don't know how to buy them, (which I suspect is far more complicated than it needs to be). I suppose the easiest way to describe what people do where I work is with an example. The chap who occasionally sits opposite me (among other things) makes sure the lead aprons hospitals buy for their radiographers are of sufficient quality that their testicles and ovaries are not being irradiated on a daily basis. We also make sure beds and so on will fit through doors, furniture matches (and isn't a breeding ground for infection) and that all rooms that require them have bins.

The next time you're in a hospital and you see a bin? Just think of me.

I can't really think of a more apposite way to end this deplorable attempt at a foreword, so I'll just leave it at that. You may form your own opinions of me based on the rest of this book which you so wisely decided to buy and I so fervently hope you enjoy reading. I mean, I already like you loads for adding it to your basket – let's hope it becomes a mutual thing.

Preparation

If you're going to tell a story or give an account of an event, it can be hard to know where to begin. People say (helpfully) to start at the beginning, which is good advice if you can say for sure when that was. A lot of the time, ideas develop from conversations that took place months – occasionally years – in the past, often in the pub after alcohol has been taken. Sometimes you have to plan so far ahead just to make the necessary bookings. Suffice to say, some activities take a fair bit of organising, with the activity itself often just the tip of the iceberg in terms of effort for group leaders.

This was an Explorer Scout trip. We are the second top section (in terms of age) in the Scout Association's structure, with ages ranging from 14 to 18. And because our members are a bit older, we get a bit more latitude around what we can do. I wish I could say since members are older they are more sensible and able; individually, they probably are, but as a group, sometimes they regress a little. When, for example, our group embarks on a trip during which they have to feed themselves, they can struggle. But since I live mostly on a diet of toast and think switching the oven on is pushing the boat out, I can't really talk.

For this year's main trip, our aim was to travel to Fort William, walk from there to Fort Augustus over three days on the Great Glen Way, then spend another four days driving round the north and west coasts of Scotland. We'd be doing it in two Land Rover Discoveries decked out to look rugged and purposeful – it was going to be nothing if not photogenic. The plan was to use British Waterway campsites during the walk, then a mixture of wild camping, not-so-wild camping and hostels for the rest of the week, all to be confirmed as we went. This was an adventure; we'd pull up at a sandy bay, park our Land Rovers just so, pitch our tents and watch the sun go down. I'd worry about how to make toast with no toaster, and the young people (of which there were eight) would boil water for their Pot Noodles and smear the 'Choco Fluff' substance they'd found on a supermarket shelf on cheap bread – it was going to be hardcore.

Except for the menu, that's not really how it worked out.

Rugged Land Rovers… Grrr…

When I buy a car, there is only one prerequisite: it needs to be shit. I don't buy good cars, I might purchase one that looks okay, but it will inevitably turn in to a car which is most definitely not good. It's hard to know if the cars I buy are bad to begin with, or if some divine power steps in and makes it so after I drive them away. If I had the means, I could buy the most reliable brand new car on the market and within a matter of milliseconds turn it into a massive pile of junk. I won't crash or drive it harshly – fate will simply look down on the transaction, shake its head ruefully and cast its spell. As warning lights begin to come on and black smoke billows from beneath the bonnet, I'll declare to whoever is interested, 'I'm not putting it in a garage, I'll fix it myself...', then embark upon an eye-wateringly expensive automotive odyssey which, nine times out of ten, just makes things worse. I know so many random things about so many obscure cars and have so many exotic single use tools that if I chose to go into any detail about them, I'd immediately be labelled The Most Boring Bastard Ever and no one would want to speak to me ever again – except perhaps to ask what kind of car I was driving, so they'd know what to avoid.

With that in mind, you can imagine my trepidation as I bought the Land Rover I would be using. We hatched a plan: I'd get my friend and fellow leader, Lewis, to buy the car. I'd give him my credit card and he'd go and buy it – that way hopefully fate or whatever higher power that over sees such things would never know. Lewis would drive it back nonchalantly, as if it were his own, and leave the keys in the ignition (and my credit card somewhere secure). Some time later I'd find it and say, 'Oh, hello, what a nice car,' and quietly adopt it as my own. That probably sounds like a lot of superstitious waffle, and I'd agree completely, so I picked a car and bought it myself.

I can't afford a brand new Land Rover. I can't even afford one that used to be nearly new, so I bought one that hadn't been new for fourteen years or so. I know you're thinking that's ancient, so of course it'll break down, but my last car was only four years old when I bought it, and it died aged only seven after a measly three years of ownership. It doesn't matter what I buy, it will break down. I convinced myself that if I spent £2000 (say) on an older car, as opposed to more on a newer one, at least I'd be limiting the inevitable losses when things begin to go wrong – as they most assuredly would. I couldn't do anything about it breaking down – I mean, I knew it would. All anyone can do is hope that whatever falls off, snaps or stops working won't be heart-attack expensive to fix. I also wondered if my car buying paradigm was all wrong, perhaps instead of concentrating on buying cars that won't break down, (because that clearly wasn't working), I might try and buy a car I believed would definitely break down. It must be said, the Land Rover Discovery confidently ticks that box. Suffice to say, it made no difference. It ended up being no better or worse than any other heap of crap I'd ever bought. I am a car killer. I am to automotive reliability what The Most Boring Bastard Ever is to the chat at dinner parties.

Lewis already had a Land Rover, and it helps that he's a mechanic, although not even his skill and experience is a match for my pestilence around cars. He'd modified his: raised the suspension and stuck huge wheels on it. We'd recently been to Arran in it and although it had a rudimentary exhaust and one or two holes in the floor (made evident by the cabin filling with blue smoke periodically) it had been reliable. I drove my new purchase back from the garage without drama but soon after fate took an interest and things started to occur.

The car started to overheat. No problem, just a leak in the coolant system – an easy fix. Poking around under the bonnet, we discovered this Land Rover was chipped, that is, it had been modified to produce more oomph. I had bought an agricultural pimp-wagon. Unfortunately, apart from getting nods from other chavs on the road, it also meant the standard coolant pipes were prone to exploding. We replaced the damaged pipe with a handsome blue silicone substitute. Although I only needed one pipe, I had to buy the whole set as, obviously, I also only buy cars whose parts are awkward and expensive to replace.

Lewis then announced his Land Rover's MOT would run out the week before the trip but would only need a bit of welding. I had trust. Lewis knows his cars – he didn't seem worried so neither was I. However, my car promptly broke down again: the key fob stopped working (which might sound trivial, but it immobilised the entire car) then the completely unnecessary-in-the-first-place *Land Rover Active Cornering Enhancement System* failed (hilariously called the ACE system – it is most assuredly not ace.) The car still drove, but I was told if I didn't have it rectified, something would probably seize or explode (or both), which may seem shocking, but I'm used to hearing that about cars I own. When the key fob stopped working, I assumed the worst. If something mechanical goes wrong on a car, usually you can see or hear what has come apart, fallen off or worn away, and while it might be awkward, at least you can see what to fix. If the electronics start playing up, the car looks and sounds exactly the same but could be mortally wounded. It's happened before – to me as it happens…

The key fob stopped working late on a Sunday night miles away from home. The train I might have caught had been cancelled and the replacement bus service was more imaginary than real. A journey that in a car would have taken 25 minutes took 90 minutes – I spent so long on one bus I'm positive the driver was going round in circles just to reinforce my deep dislike of public transport. It turned out only to be the battery in the key fob, and while I had a mild panic about the active cornering enhancement thingy, a local Land Rover specialist sorted the problem and disaster was averted. No one as yet has managed to fix the replacement bus service. I feel sure, somewhere, that bus is still doing lazy circuits around Edinburgh's outskirts, with the driver keeping his beady eyes peeled for anyone who might think public transport is an effective way to get from A to B late on a Sunday evening.

Although the Land Rover Discovery TD5 has two seats in the boot, we weren't planning to use them as we needed all the boot space for equipment and bags. However, total numbers eventually clicked over from ten to eleven which meant some poor soul would need to squeeze in, which in turn meant we'd need to get a roof rack and a roof box. Quite a lot of time and money later the afore-mentioned items were procured, so you can imagine my reaction when Lewis sent a text to say his car wouldn't pass an MOT. It turned out the welding it required needed welding, and then that welding needed to be welded too. I don't wish to sound like a car-bore, but if we used it, we would have been able to stick our feet out the bottom and power it by running.

At first I felt smug because although I knew my car would have broken down again at some point, it at least made it to the starting line. But then there was relief because it meant we'd have to hire a minibus, which we'd be doing from another Scout group. This provided a number of benefits, which were, in no particular order: a) if it broke down, they'd need to organise a replacement, b) it solved our developing space problem, and c) it would have their name plastered all over it, meaning they'd get the blame if (for example) we decided to embark upon a crime spree.

With our departure looming, we had to tweak our plans for day one. We had intended to walk the short distance between Neptune's Ladder (near Fort William) to our first night's camp at Gairlochy, a distance of eight miles or so. But because we were now picking up a minibus from some Scouting colleagues in Fife, we left a bit later and made for our first night's campsite directly, with the odd diversion along the way.

Day One – Longniddry to Gairlochy

The replacement vehicle, allowing us to travel incognito

The start of a Scout trip is always a tearful occasion: sobbing mothers tear their hair out as fathers stand by watery-eyed yet stoic. As the eldest children are ripped from the familial fold, younger siblings cry in the mud at parent's feet all but forgotten in the horror…sorry, that's not what actually happens…let me start again…

The start of a Scout trip is always a joyous occasion: laughing mothers run fingers through their hair while fathers stand by all a-glow in anticipation of what may transpire during a week without at least one of their children's continual demands for attention. As older brothers and sisters imagine a week without being nagged by parents, younger siblings tug hopefully at sleeves and ask, 'If that minibus crashes, can I have his bedroom?' Parental behaviour lives on a wide spectrum when they're seeing kids off. The length of the trip is a factor: if it's a week, some may worry how they'll manage, although sometimes it's difficult to tell if they're worried about themselves or the kids, while others seem to have an ejector seat in the car for the purpose of firing their kids into the back of the minibus. If it's a weekend, some might plead with leaders to keep them for longer while others fret about whether or not they'll be able to get back from the weekend away they've planned before their child gets back from theirs.

It's always a bit of a last minute scramble: all the things you didn't think of and all the things you never thought you would need but now think you might, and all the things you put to one side because you wouldn't need them but might eventually end up needing. The most important thing to remember is the young people because if you begin to drive away while a young person is, for example, indisposed, it looks bad. Looking back down the driveway in the rear view mirror and seeing a concerned-looking child you're sure should be aboard standing behind a parent mouthing the words, 'Where are they going?", is in terms of parental confidence, difficult to come back from.

I'm not saying that could happen. Our members are all so uniquely memorable it would be impossible to knowingly leave anybody behind. If we did, it couldn't be anything other than a deliberate act.

Suffice to say, we pulled away from home base with everyone we should have and no one we shouldn't and left the familiarity of our home town in our wake.

The road to Fort William comes into its own once you get past Stirling, passing through Callander and into the Trossachs is always pleasant. The scenery as you drive along the Eastern shores of Loch Lubnaig is a fine balance of woodland, rocky mountain and water. You'll be aware of the stereotype around young people and scenery – that they just don't appreciate it? Well, let me say now, that stereotype is 100% true – they couldn't give a toss. I don't really remember what they talked about as we travelled during the week. I know the language they used was English because I recognised individual words. However, I don't know what information they were sharing. There is also a stereotype around older people – to do with them not understanding young people. I can say this is absolutely true, but the misunderstanding is not on our side, it's on theirs because they talk a lot of nonsense to each other. These young people are to a one thoroughly decent, entertaining and pleasant to be around and when they're talking to leaders, we understand and enjoy what they're saying. When they're talking to each other though, it seems to be complete gibberish.

The leader team for this trip consisted of me: 40 years old, appreciates good scenery and out of touch with the youth of today; Lewis: 24, a mechanic by trade, single with some understanding of the things young people talk about and Michael: 18, new school leaver, freshly elevated to a leadership role and still quite young with a well rounded understanding of the burning issues affecting the youth of today. He was very much our missing link during the week, and was able to translate a lot of the chat amongst the young people for me. Lewis said he didn't understand what they were talking about, but I'm sure I saw him nod or smile knowingly during some conversations. It was nice of him to try and make me feel less marginalised. Michael made no such efforts – he was right in there with the chat about wizards, urban dictionaries and memes from the many endlessly exciting social media platforms available these days.

If you're driving to Fort William on the A82, it would be abnormal not to turn in at The Green Welly Stop at Tyndrum. It's a bit of a destination by itself, popular with coach parties, motor cyclists and the travel weary in general. There is a café, outdoor shop, whisky shop, filling station and some very busy toilets. I'm not being glib or filthy, but lots of coach parties mean lots of OAPs, ergo the toilets go like a fair.

Pretty much everything from a slice of cake to the elaborate ornamentation on display is overpriced. The bronze stags for example are about £400; that's a hell of an impulse buy to make on the way to or from the toilets. An eccentric American might go for it but how will they get a two-foot bronze stag back on the plane? They look really heavy – it would need a seat to itself. The 'sale rail' in the outdoor shop is a fright waiting to happen – customers familiar with normal high street prices will find it hard to see any savings.

In between the tourist shops and the filling station, you'll find a smaller takeaway establishment. They sell the nicest homemade Bakewell tart I've ever had the pleasure to cram into my gob – it's delicious, worth the price tag and a lot easier to deal with than a bronze stag.

The most interesting thing about The Green Welly Stop isn't the goods they have for sale, it's the people perusing them – it's such a wild mix. Miserable OAPs, gaily dressed Americans, queue jumping Spaniards and oddly dressed Germans. Then there are the bikers who sit outside looking a bit like slightly-past-their-best Power Rangers, sipping tea out of Styrofoam cups and puffing on roll-up cigarettes, and of course the ubiquitous outdoor activities people overflowing with vim, energy and zips. I find the latter group intimidating with mountain bikes strapped to complicated roof racks, trousers with too many pockets and hats with silly ear flaps. They have boundless energy. They don't just look round the shops, they form beachheads and invade them, fingering materials and examining stitching with a critical eye. Theirs is a world of ripstop nylon, Thinsulate insulation, Gore-Tex boots and breathable membranes – that last item is the unicorn of outdoor equipment. The idea that a garment will keep the rain out but allow air to leave and return thus keeping the wearer fresh and sweet-smelling is just not true. It's either waterproof and the wearer will be sweaty or it's not waterproof and you'll need to make other arrangements if you wish to remain dry. When they're done doing all of that, they stride energetically back to rugged SUVs via the nearest mountain top just because they can. It's possible the words you've just read are fuelled mostly by envy; I'd quite like to be one of those able outdoorsy people traversing rock faces with ruddy good humour. Unfortunately, when out on the hills, I resemble a tramp who mugged a hill walker.

The West Highland Way bisects Tyndrum and passes right by a more moderately priced shop called Brodies Mini-market which you can find over a foot bridge past The Green Welly Stop. Disappointingly, it's been rebranded as a 'KeyStore Express' so now sports the eye-jarring blue and yellow livery of said chain of shops. You should probably go there instead of The Green Welly Stop though. Brodies started out in the area as a mobile shop way back in 1931; it's a third generation business which is often overlooked because of how prominent The Green Welly Stop is. It's also the last shop on the West Highland Way until you get to Kinlochleven some 28 miles away across Rannoch Moor, up the Devil's Staircase and past the Blackwater Reservoir. It also has on the premises a post office, which is handy if you don't want to buy a plane ticket for your new bronze stag.

Leaving Tyndrum and its various delights behind, you pass the road for Oban and the Isles to the west; to the north, the road to Fort William makes its way along one side of a long valley toward Bridge of Orchy. If you look to your right you can see the route of the West Highland Way and the West Highland Railway Line, widely held to be one of Europe's most scenic railway journeys. If you're walking the West Highland Way, this seven mile stretch from Tyndrum to Bridge of Orchy is particularly challenging. Bearing in mind you'll already have walked 53 miles to Tyndrum, seeing the route stretch away as far as the eye can see is not a little dispiriting. To also see cars filled with warm contented people zinging along the road who will get to Fort William a full three days ahead of you (unless you're one of those outdoor activities types who might jog the ninety eight mile route for light exercise) is a bit annoying. I'd recommend getting the train back south from Fort William, as the reports of it being one of the most scenic are not without foundation. It's what we did when we walked it a few years ago, and it provided us with mixed feelings: on the one hand, it was tempting to be a bit smug about the people making their way along that unrelenting path in our wake, but on the other, we remembered being those people. It took us a good half day of tedious walking to cover the distance, whereas the train effortlessly gobbled it up in ten minutes. If nothing else, a decent long distance walk instils a newly invigorated respect for modern transport in a person.

The West Highland Railway Line traverses the eastern slopes of the valley from Tyndrum to its next stop at Bridge of Orchy – now bear with me for a moment – during which it tackles what is known in train enthusiast circles as the Horseshoe Curve. I include this information because it might be good for pub quizzes or getting rid of people you don't wish to speak to. Explain to them in a whiny voice that it is a railway feature that scribes a delicate sweeping horseshoe curve up one then back down the other side of a small valley at a place called Auch. The track then continues unhindered along the west-facing slopes of Beinn Dorain, an impressively pointy Munro (so named after Sir Hugh Munro who made the first meaningful register of mountains rising to 3000ft or more above sea level) that rises to a height of 3530ft (or 1073m if you prefer) above sea level. It's a well known feature in railway circles and since you now also know of it, if you judge me, you are a terrible hypocrite.

Next up on the road north is Bridge of Orchy, a small hamlet at the base of the col between Beinn Dorainn and Beinn an Dothaidh – if you want to climb these Munros you'd set off from here. There is a train station and a hotel with a reasonably priced bunkhouse attached, although we noticed in passing that the buildings behind the picture postcard white-washed hotel had changed. We thought perhaps they'd improved the bunkhouse; unfortunately, they've knocked it down and extended the hotel. The West Highland Way also passes through here, and the lack of cheap accommodation could prove problematic if you're not keen on splashing out on a hotel room. As it was, we just whizzed through in our minibus toward Loch Tulla and Rannoch Moor.

And what can one say about Rannoch Moor? It is quite possibly the most picturesque place in all of the British Isles. Covering some 50 square miles (or 130 square kilometres), this was one of the last places to thaw out after the last ice age, which occurred during what geologists call the Younger Dryas. (Why is so much in geology so obscurely named?) The glacier (often called the Loch Lomond Stadial) that covered Rannoch Moor and most of everything else was so heavy that since it melted 12,000 or so years ago, the land still rises by two or three millimetres every year. The ground is so waterlogged that the West Highland Railway Line sits atop a 23-mile-long floating platform of tree roots, logs, brush and much more besides – without which it would eventually sink. More over, the entire moor is a Special Area of Conservation having within its borders the Rannoch Rush, a herbaceous perennial plant – try to contain your self – only found on Rannoch Moor. Not only that, but it is also one of the few remaining locations where one can find the narrow-headed ant – you'd think an ant with a narrow head (so able to get between the tightest of cracks) would do quite well, but apparently not.

But listen, I've saved the best till last: for somewhere on Rannoch Moor, in an area called Dismal Downs one can find the fabled Castle McDuck, the ancestral home of Clan McDuck and old Scrooge McDuck himself. Whenever I travel across the moor, I always pause to drink in the moody atmosphere of the place, to let the brooding silence wash over me. You can still feel the land exhaling as it recovers from the violent weight of the Lomond Stadial ice sheet, a formation from a different epoch yet still having an effect today. I often wonder in those precious contemplative moments, as the preternatural silence settles upon my soul like the gentle caress of a familiar hand, whether Scrooge McDuck had similar thoughts as he gazed out from his castle's formidable battlements.

Joking aside, Rannoch Moor is a unique place. If you can put the busy road out of your mind, there is something about the place – it's not just one of Scotland's most photogenic locations, it is also a truly special place.

The superlative scenery doesn't stop there. Rannoch Moor is mostly undisturbed; the road skims along its surface to exit via the brooding grandeur of Glen Coe, home of the Glen Coe MacDonalds – at least until they gave shelter to 120 or so men of the Earl of Argyll's Regiment of Foot. The long running dispute between the Campbells and MacDonalds didn't arise from what transpired early on the morning of the 13th of January 1692; the feud had been simmering for centuries. But a number of the Earl's men were Campbells and it didn't help that the commander was a Campbell too, although, since he was related to the Glen Coe MacIains by marriage (at the time, the 12th chief of Clan McDonald was a MacIain), relations were amicable.

In 1688, the Glorious Revolution put William of Orange on the English throne, ousting James II of England who for many was still James VII of Scotland. The Scottish Parliament of the day took a cautious approach to the appointment. They wrote to James and to William asking for assurances but were ultimately disappointed with the responses – James advised the Scottish Clans to accept William as their new king. This led to early Jacobite uprisings in the first instance led by John Graham, 1st Viscount of Dundee ostensibly to return James VII to the English throne. Jacobite forces won at Killiecrankie – fought on the 27th of July 1689 - but Viscount Bonnie Dundee, as Graham was also known, was killed. The Jacobite army was then defeated by Cameronian forces during the battle of Dunkeld in August of 1689, then again more heavily at the Haughs of Cromdale in May of 1690. Finally, Jacobite soldiers fighting along side Irish Catholics and several regiments of French troops were defeated by William at the Battle of the Boyne in July 1690 – the effects of that battle can still be felt today. James left for exile in France under something of a cloud among Irish fighters who felt he'd lost his nerve after the battle.

A pardon was offered to Highland Clans for their part in the Jacobite uprisings conditional on them swearing an oath of allegiance before the 1st of January 1692. Highland chiefs sent word to their King-in-exile who dithered because he fancied he could make a return. Reality dictated otherwise and Clan Chiefs eventually took the oath to King William.

With time already running out, Alastair MacIain, 12th Chief of Glencoe, set out for Fort William to take the oath. (If you are wondering why the 12th Chief of Glencoe was a MacIain and not a MacDonald, the MacIains of Glencoe were a branch of Clan MacDonald. In texts they are often referred to as the MacDonalds of Glencoe – they're interchangeable.) On arrival he was told no one there was authorised to receive it and was instructed to go to Inveraray and see the Sheriff of Argyle, Sir Colin Campbell. Even though MacIain carried with him a letter of protection and another confirming he had arrived to swear his allegiance within the specified time, he was still detained by soldiers from the 1st company of the Earl of Argyle's Regiment of Foot under the command of one Captain Drummond. Finally arriving at Inveraray, MacIain had to wait another three days because – not wishing to sound flippant – Sir Colin wasn't in.

Eventually, Sir Colin did accept Alastair MacIain's oath.

Unfortunately, it wasn't enough. At that point there was a coming together of mutual agendas: Secretary of State for Scotland and Lord Advocate John Dalrymple Master of Stair – a lowlander who had a dislike for highlanders and their way of life – John Campbell 1st Earl of Breadalbane and Holland and Archibald Campbell 10th Earl of Argyle, both senior members of the Campbell clan. John Dalrymple already had a plan to break the clans, a system he despised enthusiastically. Alastair MacIain's oath was declared null and void, and Dalrymple persuaded King William to sign an order meant to 'root out a den of thieves' in the valley of Glen Coe that would see the MacDonalds of Glen Coe 'extirpated'.

Much is made of the hospitality of the highlanders and not without cause. In terrible winter conditions, days prior to the massacre, they took in the soldiers who as far as the clans-people knew were there to collect taxes. Captain Robert Campbell of Glen Lyon and his 120 men may not have known the real reason for being there – he had legitimate orders from Colonel Hill to collect a new tax recently levied. Hill was the Governor of Fort William who supplied MacIain with letters of support on his way to Inveraray – it was hoped this would alleviate any suspicions the MacIains of Glen Coe may have had.

On the 12th of February Captain Drummond arrived with new orders.

You are hereby ordered to fall upon the rebells, the McDonalds of Glenco, and put all to the sword under seventy. you are to have a speciall care that the old Fox and his sones doe upon no account escape your hands, you are to secure all the avenues that no man escape. This you are to putt in execution att fyve of the clock precisely; and by that time, or very shortly after it, I'll strive to be att you with a stronger party: if I doe not come to you att fyve, you are not to tarry for me, but to fall on. This is by the Kings speciall command, for the good & safety of the Country, that these miscreants be cutt off root and branch. See that this be putt in execution without feud or favour, else you may expect to be dealt with as one not true to King nor Government, nor a man fitt to carry Commissione in the Kings service. Expecting you will not faill in the full-filling hereof, as you love your selfe, I subscribe these with my hand att Balicholis Feb: 12, 1692.

For their Majesties service

Although Captain Robert Campbell of Glen Lyon some years before had land looted by the MacIains from Glen Coe and their cousins from Glen Garry, he did not seem overly exercised about it – he was comfortable sitting with Alastair MacIain for dinner over the course of two weeks. Unfortunately, Campbell's presence enabled the conspirators to present the massacre as a local problem between warring clans.

In any event, MacIain was slain as he tried to rise from his bed. In all, 38 men were murdered in their homes or while trying to flee. Forty women and children died of exposure because their homes had been burned to the ground. Some of the soldiers managed to warn their hosts: Lieutenants Francis Farquhar and Gilbert Kennedy smashed their weapons rather than use them on their unsuspecting hosts. They were imprisoned but later exonerated; they also gave evidence against their officers during the enquiry that followed.

In addition to the men already staying with the MacDonalds, two more detachments of around 400 men each were supposed to converge on the valley: one from Kinlochleven via the Devil's Staircase (now part of the West Highland Way) and the others from the south. They didn't make their positions on time, either because of the weather or because they didn't want to be involved in what they knew would be a slaughter.

After the enquiry, blame was laid at the feet of the Secretary of State for Scotland, Lord Advocate John Dalrymple (Master of Stair.)

Recommendations were made but in the end no action was taken, which might sound familiar. There are differing opinions about how much King William knew. They range from him being duped completely by John Dalrymple to him being wholly in charge and responsible. Either way what we do know is there has never been a shortage of Scots who were prepared to do their own people a mischief for advancement, sway or riches – it was true then and, arguably, still true today.

There is a haunting song written by Jim MacLean called The Ballad of Glen Coe. It is often mistaken for a traditional Scottish folk song so out of copyright, but it was written only forty-odd years ago. I'd share the lyrics with you here but it would be more effective (and less litigious) if you searched for them online.

There are some who claim Glen Coe has an eeriness to it, a certain sadness. It's a wind blasted desolate place, and on a day when the weather is poor it makes for grim mental imagery to think of women and children perishing in the snow. It's also incredibly grand in terms of scale and – assuming you can tune out the coach parties – it can be an oddly oppressive place. The mountains running down either side of Glen Coe are not verdant pudding bowl shaped hills – they are harsh and unforgiving with steep rocky faces running down into fields of scree dotted with boulders. The mountains on either side are not to be treated lightly; especially the northern peaks which make one of Scotland's finest and most exhilarating ridge walks, the Aonach Eagach. If you lose your footing, you won't find yourself rolling and giggling down a pleasant grassy slope, you'll fall screaming to your death. Even when you land you'll still have hundreds of feet to roll and bounce.

Some time ago, with a different group of Scouts, it took us three attempts to complete the ridge walk. In hindsight, doing it with a novice group was a little fool hardy. It's not necessary to get roped up although in places you would certainly think otherwise. As we gingerly crabbed our way along, picking our hand and footholds with care, other groups skipped past with annoying surefootedness. At one point – and its important to understand the route is not well defined so we might not have had to go this way – we were all sitting astride a long sharp ridge with legs dangling out over dizzying drops. The person in front of me had a mild panic attack which set me off. I didn't embarrass myself too badly, and the mountain rescue team were very sympathetic – I'm joking, we had a moment from which we both recovered, then we found our way down to safety and agreed to never to do anything so stupid ever again.

At the western end of Glen Coe you'll find the Clachaig Inn and the villages of Glen Coe and Ballachulish. The Clachaig Inn, so called because it sits near to the bottom of the dangerous Clachaig Gully, is a popular place with outdoor sorts. Sitting in the back bar on a busy Friday or Saturday night, it's hard to know where all the people come from. It can sit quite empty, then all of a sudden fill up with rowdy people, then be quiet again – it reminds me of a musical performance in a film (bear with me). You know what I mean: it's a perfectly normal scene but you know a song is brewing, and all of a sudden people start prancing about whooping and crooning, then just as suddenly, they're back to normal as if none of it ever happened, and so it is in the Clachaig's back bar. From no where, colourful people appear in the bar, richly attired and smiling, holding drinks – some may even be singing. Then, they all steal away into the night leaving nothing in their wake except the faint smell of booze and one lonely, abandoned Puffa jacket.

I should tell you a story that always makes me smile. Unfortunately, you probably had to be there, but listen, I'm going to tell you anyway – you have free will, so skip ahead if you like. A friend of mine was staying with his family in one of the Clachaig Inn cabins. His name is Sheridan and sometimes he can be a bit of an idiot. I can't lie, when this occurred it was late in the evening and alcohol had been and indeed was still being consumed. We were sitting out at a picnic bench when across the car park a very proud, very large stag emerged from the tree line. Sheridan, who fancies himself as something of a photographer, produced an iPhone and got up to approach the untamed mammal. He was doing quite well despite my telling him it was a dangerous wild animal so probably best left alone. As he was finding a good spot from which to snap a photo, I decided it might be prudent to put something substantial between myself and the wild beast; unfortunately, in doing so it may have seemed to the stag as if we were trying to corner it. I made it to a sturdy looking tree a good twenty feet from what was now a mildly concerned stag (we knew it was mildly concerned from its body language – it was snorting and pawing the ground like a bull). Meanwhile (as I distracted it with my inexplicable pincer movement) Sheridan had managed to close with the now quite agitated beast – he couldn't have been more than fifteen feet away. Delicately holding the phone in that way people do, he dabbed at the screen with a finger causing the flash to activate. It was a moment of visceral fear, for all involved. The stag dropped its head and made to charge, but instead, pulled up at the last millisecond and held its antlers low ready to gore. I can say without hesitation, I've never seen a human being move as fast as Sheridan did – even then that isn't strictly accurate because I didn't actually see him move as such.

One moment he was standing with his phone held aloft in front of this iconic and currently wild-eyed Scottish mammal, the next he's fifty feet away peering from behind a large wheely bin – he'd managed to somehow teleport himself between the two points. The stag then turned its attention and antlers to me, and with terrified eyes and flared nostrils (the stag, not me) it began to advance in single angry stomps, antlers menacingly jabbing with each step. All of a sudden the tree I was cowering behind seemed quite flimsy. This wasn't a moment of fright, it was a dawning realisation that I was going to be gored by an angry, pissed off stag, and would be forever known as 'that drunk guy who got attacked by a stag'. I'd probably make it on to ladbible.com, I'd be a Facebook meme – and

I never even started it. But just then Sheridan reappeared holding a large traffic cone to his lips, through which he issued the loudest strangest honk. I don't have adequate words to describe it. I've never seen a stag being tasered (nor do I want to) but I'd expect it to look a lot like this. It leapt into the air, tried to find the new threat while in midair, couldn't, so turned (also in mid-air) and ran crashing into the trees.

I know, it's not that funny. Perhaps it was the dichotomy between feeling near to serious injury and the bizarre sight of a grown man honking through a traffic cone at a wild stag. I have no idea what might have happened had he not reappeared equipped as he was. Sheridan claimed he was trying to reproduce the sound of a much bigger and angrier stag and who's to argue – it worked.

If you have kids who are fans of Harry Potter, it's worth noting scenes from the films were shot just up the hill a bit from the Clachaig Inn. For a while, passers-by could see Hagrid's cabin and other notable props from the films. It's also midge central which caused the film crew some problems, although it's not clear if any of the celebrities came under attack. It would be difficult to do anything, including pretending to be a wizard, while swarms of Scottish midges were on the rampage. The Scottish midge costs the tourism industry close to £300 million per year, or so they say – I'm never sure how they measure these things. However, their loss is Avon's gain, their Skin-So-Soft range is the current go-to insect repellent; it's even favoured by the armed forces. In truth, when conditions are perfect, usually around water at dusk when the air is still, nothing stops them. Retreat indoors if you can and stay there.

Ballachulish village comes in three parts: Ballachulish Village itself with its old slate mine (now a popular park) then North and South Ballachulish, separated by the impressive iron-built Ballachulish Bridge. The bridge was opened in 1975, but before then, a ferry operated or travellers detoured round Loch Leven (whose narrows the bridge spans) visiting the quiet village of Kinlochleven on the way. You might expect Kinlochleven, sidelined as it was by the ferry then the bridge, to be a backwater, but its not. It is home to Scotland's only indoor ice climbing centre and 100 trillion midges during summer. The West Highland Way also winds its way down to the village after reaching its highest point (550metres or 1850ft) some way after the top of the Devil's Staircase, which coincidently is the same route used by the soldiers coming from the north in the lead-up to the massacre at Glen Coe. It's one of the most scenic parts of the route with views toward the Aonach Eagach ridge to the west, the mighty Blackwater Reservoir to the north east, water from which was used to power the now defunct aluminium smelters in Kinlochleven, and to the north, the grandeur of the Mamore Mountains and the Ring of Steel.

However, we're getting off track. We were about to drive over the Ballachulish Bridge leaving Argyle and entering Invernesshire. Since the young folk had worn themselves out appreciating all the glorious scenery – which is a notion I just made up – and we had time to spare because we wouldn't be walking from Banavie to Gairlochy that day, we decided to stop at the Corran Ferry. If you are passing the Corran Ferry (which you do if you're travelling to Fort William), it is simply the done thing to jump on as a foot passenger (which is free), go to the other side of Loch Linnhe, then come back again. Since we had some time to kill, that is what we did. The young folk are good at entertaining themselves (some of them can really talk, I mean *really* talk), but sometimes, camping can be a bit boring, so we didn't want to arrive on site too early. We were aiming to get there with enough light left in the day to put tents up and prepare a meal, after which we'd be free to poke the fire and blether late into the evening. Never underestimate the attraction of the naked flame to the young adolescent. We call fires lazy Scout attractors; you could set a fire and Scouts – any child probably – will arrive from impressive distances as if by magic to poke it with a stick. It is a universal constant and must be a biological imperative developed in days of yore when Homo sapiens roamed the plains living on instinct alone – and that instinct was telling them to find a fire to poke.

The Corran Ferry – there's also a nice pub on the other side of the water if you feel inclined

But anyway, the Corran Ferry: it's round the headland past the small settlement of Onich. It's a small car ferry that cuts a sizeable corner if you're travelling west of Fort William or to the UK mainland's most westerly point at Ardnamurchan. If you're not doing that though, you can still get on the ferry as a foot passenger and go for a cup of tea at the Corran Inn in the village across the water. The port on the mainland side is called Ardgour but the ferry has always been named after the village on the west. The crossing only takes fifteen or twenty minutes. When the tide is strong it can be an interesting experience – the ferry is forced to crab its way across the surging tidal waters, struggling to stay within the Corran Narrows.

It was getting on for mid afternoon when the ferry returned, happily with all the Explorers it left with. We reboarded our borrowed minibus, which was beginning to show hints of a hard life, and got back on the road for Fort William. The idea was to have a look round the town centre then do some food shopping. We needed to buy dinner for that night plus supplies for the following day, bearing in mind we'd need packed lunches too. Catering whilst out and about depends on several things. If they're a younger group they tend to need a little more supervision, Scouts (aged 10 to 14) often aren't practical. It's usually pizza or McDonalds –the former can't reasonably be done without an oven and the latter we try to eschew. So we compromise. We accompany them to the shops to make sure they buy practical stuff then show them what to do with it, or in my case, recuse myself and let someone else show them what to do. With Explorers, you might think they're better able to cope. Individually, they probably are, but none are keen to take the lead. That said, once they get going, they're easily as competent, and in some cases, even more competent than me. I'm not saying I've ever cooked pasta in the kettle, but I still don't know why you can't … just tape the button down and monitor the situation … it saves on pans too…

Here's an example: some time ago, twelve of us were away for the weekend, staying in an outdoor centre – just us mind, so we had the place to ourselves. We stopped at a large superstore on the way and sent Explorers in with cash to buy food for the weekend. We'd discussed the menu at length so we were, as they say, all on the same page. Two main meals, two breakfasts and three lunches plus snacks (within reason), how hard could it be? I should say this was a previous generation of Explorers, not the current batch, although Michael was an Explorer at the time, so shares some of the responsibility. What came out of the shop was the very basic makings of what we'd discussed, that is, the absolute minimum limit of what I would have bought (usual caveats apply) and about £100 worth of Pringles, Doritos and Irn Bru. Perched on top of it all were several bags of finger rolls which I picked up questioningly. 'Are we having hotdogs?' I asked. 'No,' they said, 'it's instead of rolls. Did you know they're half the price of rolls?' I said I did and suggested they might be half the price because they're half the size.

No one has bought finger rolls since.

The nature of the activity also has a bearing. If you're carrying everything or are pushed for space, you'll be using light weight technical cooking gear only really good for cooking for two or three people at a time. The food you buy also has to be considered. Dried food can seem attractive in terms of weight saving and is fine so long as water is readily available, but if it isn't, you have to carry it in with you, and as you might imagine, anything that needs an oven is off the menu. I'll be honest, this isn't my strong suit. Purists might frown, but I tend toward tinned food: stews, curries or chilli and maybe some tinned veg, and if I'm feeling audacious, I might even boil some rice. We have in the past tried 'proper' outdoor food – pre-prepared meals that come in thick foil boil-in-the-bag packaging. They're tasty in the same way an entire packet of Jaffa Cakes is tasty

– it's quite satisfying at the time, but afterwards you're left feeling a bit dirty and perhaps a wee bit guilty. So many things in life can be likened to a one night stand and specialist outdoor food is no exception – like some one night stands, they can be quite expensive and not particularly satisfying.

But I digress.

On our trip, we were somewhere in between. Space was limited so we were using lightweight equipment but since the van was shadowing walkers along the route, they didn't have to carry all their kit. We didn't have to worry too much about what food we bought, so long as it fitted in the small pan sets we were using. We had no oven but we had enough space for a small double burner on which we could use larger pans. The leader team mostly took advantage of the double burner, while the young people split into smaller groups and used lightweight stoves with the technical pot sets. As the week progressed: more and more of what we were preparing on the big cooker was being eaten by Explorers, which was fine by us.

Normally leaders would hold on to budgets for food but again, with the older sections, nurturing responsibility and independence is something of an objective. What better way to do that than to allow them to set their own budgets and choose their menu accordingly. To give the group their due, they were incredibly thrifty, but mostly because they hardly bought any food. At first we thought perhaps they didn't know what to buy, but after a quick leader confab, we decided it was an issue of confidence. We've seen this before; within the group no one wants to take the lead for fear of criticism. They have good ideas but keep quiet in case the group decide they're rubbish – there is no reason to this process, it can be cruelly arbitrary. This is a common refrain for Scout Leaders. We frequently ask for suggestions and ideas about where to go and things to do, but once the cries of skydiving, powerboat racing and discussions about where the nearest bordello is have died down, no one really wants to stick their neck out for fear of being lambasted. In the absence of realistic suggestions, leaders end up picking activities and if we pick wrongly, we never hear the end of it. And so it was with food. From what I understand they set a budget which was fine but couldn't reach a consensus on what to buy. Some did try to take the lead but were shouted down or ignored, so the resulting purchases seemed to be an uneasy compromise between what they thought an adult and a eight-year-old child might buy. Lunches were easy, sandwiches or rolls, cartons of juice, crisps and biscuits and perhaps a bit of fruit – purely as an afterthought. All of that coupled with the confectionary they were buying with their own cash meant they didn't starve during the day. Breakfast was also easy, although they did get stuck in the cereal-and-bacon-roll rut, which was a shame for Explorer Harry who didn't eat meat. Because cereal is generally taken with milk, it's not a practical breakfast when camping. It's also dish intensive, takes up too much space and let's be honest, without proper cooling arrangements, eating cereal made soggy by warm milk is similar to eating vomit. I should point out, I don't make a habit of eating vomit so I don't know this for a fact – I'm merely painting a picture with words. Cereal bars on the other hand are far more practical, so we bought a great many of those – so many, we became sick of them by the end of the week.

In any case, we sent them off to wander round Morrisons, and every now and again we'd catch a glimpse of them loitering at the far end of an aisle stuffing items into pockets – I'm joking. Mostly they just milled about looking unsure of themselves while occasionally picking up something their parents would never in a million years buy during a food shop.

After a dubious time at Fort William's main supermarket, we moved on to our first campsite at Gairlochy. We'd camped here before so knew what to expect. What we weren't sure of was if the keys we'd bought three years ago would still work in the canal toilet blocks. While it wasn't as cold or wet as when we last stayed, not having access to the toilets and showers would have meant a trip to the Canal Office at Corpach near Fort William to buy more keys. They're a handy resource, being as they are warm and clean. We tried our keys in all the doors, which opened as they should. Between victorious whoops and spontaneous US-style applause, we cast a critical eye over the amenities until we realised we were essentially hanging around some toilets, at which point we decided, grudgingly, to leave. It's tempting you see, to just stay in the toilets or laundry room; they're warm and dry with hot and cold running water and if you do need to go… Unfortunately, we didn't think the yachting types who also use these amenities would appreciate having to step round several bodies to put a washing on. We also weren't sure encouraging a group of teenagers to sleep in a toilet wouldn't merit a mention on a register; we didn't want to chance it.

The campsite was as we remembered, on the northern side of the locks with picnic tables and a couple of fire pits. The ground was as rocky as we remembered under the grass, making it hard to guy our tents out properly, but this time we pitched our tents away from the trees. Three years ago we pitched beneath them and slept on thinly covered tree roots, which was deeply uncomfortable even with Thermarests deployed. Despite the ground, the tents went up quickly and were ready for occupancy just as it got fully dark. Once personal kit was stowed, we set about cooking dinner. Leaders had selected for their meal a fine penne pasta bolognese, cooked by my fair hand – frankly, I'm surprised it was edible. The kids on the other hand dined less luxuriantly; dinner for them consisted of tomato soup and Pot Noodles. A mug of soup and a pot of sawdust isn't really enough and while they had plenty junk food to cover, it's no substitute for a decent hot meal. We looked at our pot of pasta bolognese and considered having seconds then maybe thirds, then looked at the young folk with their sunken eyes and empty bowls. We looked again at our still-full pots and contemplated our consciences. Eventually we decided we couldn't stand idly by and allow the situation to continue. They were obviously all still famished and the site of the fragrant wholesome food was clearly upsetting them, so we did the only decent thing and selflessly risked indigestion by quickly finishing it off.

Of course, I'm joking. Even my cooking wasn't enough to put them off – it was like that scene in Oliver as they timidly approached with their bowls. That set the routine for the week, and although we tried to give some instructions on food quantities, if I'm being honest, we weren't much better. I'd like to say we usually had plenty left over because we knew they wouldn't have enough. The truth is we had plenty left over because we were doing the opposite of the kids and buying too much.

With dinner dishes done after the usual amounts of persuasion – I was going to make a pithy comment about them wondering where their parents would appear from, but I think they all have dishwashers at home – we settled in for the night. It was certainly cold enough to merit a fire so we foraged for fallen wood and built up a respectable pile. Some of the young folk decided it would be warmer, if a lot less sociable, to go to bed, possibly the only thing that could attract an adolescent away from an open fire. Sitting round a cheerful blaze late into the night is one of the more enjoyable things to do while camping, and frankly, I'm not sure why anyone wouldn't want to do it. The warmth and the discussions to be had allow everyone to get to know each other properly. Times like these mean the difference between leaders being regarded as human, or being regarded as a robot that recharges in an alcove until the young folk next appear. From a leader's perspective, even if the young person doesn't realise it, this is the time to build good working relationships. Scouts are a uniformed youth organisation, which has its roots in a loose militaristic regimen, but because of that, barriers can appear. While some groups go down the militaristic road, I'll be honest I find it difficult to keep a straight face during all the pomp of flag break and inspection. Also, I can't wear a uniform – I just don't like it. We leave that to the younger sections where it still has value in terms of novelty and structure. The older sections, the old Venture Scout Units and now Explorers or Network, never really did it, or at least our group didn't. Sitting around the camp fire chatting away about everything and nothing is as good a way to humanise yourself, and we've found that if the young people know you as a person and not just a leader then a much better relationship develops. Bearing in mind we rely on mutual understanding and respect to get along, if they misbehave or refuse to do as they're told (not that this crowd ever do) we can't give them lines or beat the crap out of them.

I would share some of the camp fire chat from that first night but what is talked about round the camp fire, stays round the camp fire – it's a matter of trust.

In reality, it's a matter of poor memory – I can't actually remember.

Day Two – Gairlochy to Laggan Locks

The Fairy Glen in its hey day, and at its least creepy

Sunday morning greeted us with a blue sky studded with clouds, and thankfully we'd been spared a frost overnight, but the tents were damp with morning dew. I try to be first up, and you might think this is because I'm the responsible adult, the leader in charge no less, leading by example from the front and all that stuff. It's not. It's because spending the night in a hike tent in which you can barely sit up let alone stand is not conducive to a graceful start to the day. I don't want anyone to see me emerge tramp-like from my tent, clothes on back to front because I had to get dressed lying down. I also need time for my face to rearrange itself back into something approaching its normal shape instead of an imprint of whatever I was using as a pillow during the night – I tell you, camping is not all it's cracked up to be. I can wax lyrical about the power of a campfire and how it humanises those who sit round it, but it would be so much more pleasant if you had a proper bed to retire to in a space that allows you to at least stand up.

I wasn't going to include this because I am a bit embarrassed about it (in fact, I should probably form a support group). Anyway, I bought a new sleeping bag for this trip, and I was attracted to it in the shop because it advertised itself as being a bit bigger than the standard 'mummy' style bags available. It wasn't until later that it occurred to me – for all its talk of being more roomy and so better for people who 'like to move around at night', or for those 'who feel constrained by mummy sleeping bags – in NHS circles they'd call it a bariatric sleeping bag. In normal discourse you'd call it a sleeping bag for fat people. If people want to call me a bariatric Scout Leader then I suppose it's okay, at least I have freedom of movement during the night.

There is also the oft-told story of the overweight hiker emerging from his tent and a companion saying, 'I see you're tent is still up. I didn't think you bothered with the poles any more…'

In any case, the day looked to be a good one for walking, not too cold and not too warm. As the young folk dragged themselves from tents I boiled some water for coffee. I use a Trangia stove with a gas conversion kit, which I cannot recommend highly enough; you can go from nought to hot beverage in less than a minute. My only complaint is it does use a lot of gas, which can be problematic if you're planning to be self-sufficient for a long period of time. Occasionally, you might see Bear Grylls or Ray Mears squeezing the moisture out of a reindeer jobby to boil up on an open fire, but I'm glad to say we've moved on from that and while it might be good for the telly, in reality it is neither practical nor necessary. You don't even need to carry coffee, sugar and milk these days; it all comes in a handy sachet. As I did that, the young folk ambled back from the toilet blocks with hair expertly styled and clothes arranged just so. Stoves were lit, bacon soon sizzled and milk was slopped over picnic tables and the wider countryside. This is another truism about young people; educationally they are streets ahead of people like me. They can differentiate and analyse, work out the area beneath a curve and solve quadratic equations, and with the advent of console games, they have the reactions and physical poise of fighter jet pilots. We slowpokes can only watch in amazement as fingers and toes dance with pinpoint accuracy and timing across controllers that bristle with buttons, knobs and joysticks. Yet, they cannot pour milk onto cereal without also pouring it onto everything else.

We have an annual Christmas party during which we had to stop using plastic cups; we were simply wasting too much fizzy juice. The young revellers would carefully position the plastic cup on the table, unscrew the bottle top, and then, with tongue-out concentration, upend until the fizzy pop gently yet inexorably knocked the hopelessly overwhelmed cup over – meanwhile, they'd stare in frit confusion while the juice continued to flow. We'd shout and wave our arms, though by now they'd be fully mesmerised by the colourful beverage as it spread toward the edge of the table and inevitably onto the floor. We'd wail and pull our hair out (I'm exaggerating now) and as one leader dives into the kitchen for a mop, another falls to his knees and screams, 'WHY? WHY? WHY?' (I'm really exaggerating now). It's just one of those things. I can't explain it, but in twenty odd years of youth work, I've never seen a youth pour fluid into a disposable plastic cup without also pouring it over a lot of other stuff.

During last night's campfire the three leaders were imaginatively labelled Leaders Number One, Two and Three. Being in overall charge I was Leader Number One, Lewis being older than Michael was Leader Number Two and Michael being the youngest (and our link and interpreter when the young people spoke) was Leader Number Three. Today, Leader Number Two would be walking the 11 miles to Laggan Locks with the main group while Leaders One and Three picked up more supplies - while sitting round the camp fire the night before we thought we might buy a cheap gazebo and some storage boxes, the former for if it rained and the latter for organisational purposes. Because it wasn't possible to park the van near to where we were camping and due to my hatred of using poly bags while in the great outdoors, we'd pack one storage box with cooking equipment and the other with food, instead of humping several bags we need only hump (technical term meaning to carry) the two boxes. Once those items were procured, we'd continue to Laggan Locks, park the van and walk back toward the rest of the group.

Our usual routine on leaving a campsite is simple: it doesn't matter how we found it, we always leave it in a better state. With tents packed and equipment back in the van, we lined up for a litter sweep. This involves standing arms length apart in a line and slow-walking from one side of the site to the other picking up anything that shouldn't be there. It's also handy for finding tent pegs and other assorted camping paraphernalia – as a scout group we rarely have to buy metal tent pegs because we find so many of them. That said, the ground at the British Waterways campsites is so hard, it's difficult to get the pegs even halfway into the ground – which is also my only complaint about them.

Once done, Michael and I headed for the van while Lewis and the intrepid walkers headed up onto the road.

This stretch of the Great Glen Way also takes in the fabled Fairy Glen. Before going back to Fort William for supplies, we passed the walkers with a cheery toot on the horn and drove on to the unofficial visitor attraction, which is only about a mile and a half beyond Gairlochy and sits right on the Great Glen Way itself. I first found the Fairy Glen four or five years ago on a practice hike before attempting the West Highland Way. Back then the Fairy Glen was in full bloom, an area of forestry commission land given over to hundreds of stuffed toys, plastic figurines and other displays some might call cute or magical, but which I call creepy and disturbing. I still say if a person stumbled onto the place at night they'd do well to be worried. I suppose they might look for a film crew or do what people in horror films always seem to do – go and investigate only to be murdered horribly. In its heyday, it was looked after by a local woman for charity, and there was even a visitor's book and plastic tub in which you could leave a comment and some coins. People who knew it was there would return to add soft toys and other curiosities to the motley collection: stuffed animals from Disney films to free toys from fast food boxes, there was a bit of everything. Some of the displays seemed to be more macabre in nature. Take, for example, the tree which had hanging from it countless baby shoes, or another which had those super creepy porcelain Geisha masks attached – I mean, come on, if you walked into that in the middle of the night in the woods, you'd shit yourself, right?

Now though, it looked washed out and abandoned. A handwritten notice informed visitors that the area was due to be felled by the Forestry Commission. The various displays and tableaux, all the stuffed toys that had survived the years would be disposed of and the area stripped of trees. I hope it reappears somewhere else because at its height it was something to behold. You'd be walking along in the kind of daze long distance walkers are used to and suddenly through the trees a dash of colour would catch your eye. You'd assume, as I did, that it was maybe some litter or perhaps a tent, but as you closed in, the wonder/terror would build. Unfortunately, our young group missed it when it was at its best so couldn't fully grasp just how magical/disturbing it used to be. Leaders Number One, Two and Three who had visited it in its prime were somewhat disappointed on their behalf.

With the visit concluded, Michael and I trudged back up to the minibus and our chores while the walkers headed westward. The canal merges with Loch Lochy at Gairlochy so the route changes from the pleasant monotony of the canal towpath to woodland paths, a bit of black top and forestry roads above the northern banks of Loch Lochy. For us travelling back to Fort William, we passed the Commando Memorial, which sits on the main road just past Spean Bridge at the turn off for Gairlochy, and is one of the best known war memorials in Scotland and a popular tourist attraction.

Situated here in 1952 because of its proximity to Achnacarry Castle, which sits midway between the western tip of Loch Lochy and Loch Arkaig, it commemorates where the original British Commando forces trained during the Second World War, from 1942 onwards anyway. The area still has strong links with the British Commandos, the US Army Rangers and other allied Special Forces Units. The commando training at Achnacarry concluded with an 'opposed landing' on the banks of Loch Lochy not a million miles away from where the Fairy Glen is (or was) situated. Injuries were common because live ammunition was used. One wonders what those commandos would have made of the tree with the baby shoes hanging from it or the giant teddy with its coterie of stuffed toy acolytes in damp attendance. I imagine they would have slit its neck or some other terminal thing.

Achnacarry Castle is also the seat of chiefs for Clan Cameron. A small museum exists in a cottage nearby with artefacts on display from the castle and from those who lived within its walls. I should also mention it's not really a castle; the original fir-planked castle was destroyed by fire in the aftermath of the Jacobite rising in or around 1746, the new building is a Scottish baronial affair built in the early 19th century, and very fetching it is too.

As we trundled back to Fort William for our supplies, Leader Number Two and the group made their way toward Laggan Lock along the northern slopes of the Great Glen. The route continues from Achnacarry and Bunarkaig to the tiny village of Clunes (no shops) and on into forestry land on decent tracks. Walkers need to be mindful of logging trucks here; normally, there are signs posted if logging activity is taking place, but sometimes they get knocked down, be aware, the truck drivers sometimes travel at a fair lick. With our business finished in Fort William – a typically depressing visit to Argos - we headed eastwards again. The main A82 Fort William to Inverness road meanders across hillsides then drops down to the banks of Loch Lochy at a place called Letter Finlay. If we had binoculars, we might've been able to see the rest of the group ambling along the track on the other side of the sun-dappled water –

pretty much all of the forest had been felled. Instead, we used the two way radios we'd brought along to try to get in touch with them. Boasting a range of some five or six miles, we still only managed to understand the odd syllable from the broken conversation we had even though Lewis couldn't have been more than four miles distant – unless they'd got horribly lost. It was difficult to know how far along they'd got because there are no easily identifiable landmarks on the north side of Loch Lochy; the scenery was dominated mostly by tree stumps. Michael and I moved on and parked at Laggan Locks, crossed over the canal on foot at the lock gates and headed back toward the rest of the group. I did a similar thing with a previous group, of which Leader Number Three was a part, some years before and ended up walking more miles than they did. They'd made so little progress during the day that they'd only walked three of the eleven miles before we eventually reached them, meaning we had a sixteen-mile day versus their sedentary eleven. This time, Michael and I were happy to reach the rest of the group at the 'official' wild campsite that sits about three miles from Laggan Locks. When we were last here, it was just a signpost directing would-be campers down toward the loch side where space could be found to camp. Now though, the sign had been joined by a composting toilet and refuse facility; unfortunately, some idiot had vandalised both so they were out of action.

It looked like the toilet had been closed for one reason or another and some joker had decided to scratch into the woodwork how he'd travelled the length of the Great Glen Way to empty his bowels only to find the toilet facilities closed. I mean, it's not even funny to begin with, and the daft git must have thought it would be even funnier if he/she defaced the facilities. Whoever he or she is may I offer you this Scottish curse: I hope your next shite is a hedgehog. There's no need for this sort of thing – no need at all.

Turns out there are five of these 'Trailblazer' wild campsites along the Way. This one, known as Glas Dhoire, is the best appointed with its rugged open-sided shelter down by the waterside. They're aimed at canoeists mostly, with the two on Loch Ness, at Knockie and Foyers, being on the opposite side of the loch from the route of the Great Glen Way. There are camping areas at Leiterfearn on the banks of Loch Oich and at Kytra Locks on the canal about two miles short of Fort Augustus that walkers can access though. It's important to note - and this is something the arse that vandalised the toilets at Glas Dhoire may not have realised - you hire key cards from the Corpach Sea Lock Office, or its equivalent at the Inverness end, to access the composting toilets. They cost £10, but you also get access to the toilet and shower blocks we were accessing with our old keys. What I don't know is if our keys would have opened the Trailblazer composting toilets, it never occurred to us to try because I'm only reading about the Trailblazer sites now, a number of months after our trip ended. I suppose I could drive up there and revisit Glas Dhoire to check it out for you, but I don't feel we know each other well enough for such a commitment – It would feel as if I was putting in all the effort and you were just sitting there…

We followed the arrow on the happily unmolested sign down to the Loch's edge to find our group resting in the rugged-looking shelter which had been constructed since our last visit. Michael and I had brought cartons of juice, crisps and biscuits which we ate in front of the walkers – I jest, of course, we shared with the group. We could see some were not used to walking longish distances. It turned out Rhianna – our solitary-so-quite-brave female member – had borrowed her Mum's walking boots for the week. It's as well we weren't walking all week, as you really need boots you've broken in yourself. It doesn't really matter how well others might fit, as walking for days on end will magnify the tiniest bit of chafing that under normal circumstances wouldn't be noticed. The merest hint of a dropped stitch or lose flap inside the boots your wearing will become the bane of your existence after a few ten or twelve-mile days.

Socks are also worth thinking about. Buy plenty of walking socks that are high wicking, meaning they carry moisture away from the skin thus preventing blisters. Cotton socks don't wick well, as the moisture coupled with the high friction both softens then inflames the skin causing blisters to appear very quickly. It's worth spending some money on socks, but don't go daft as it is possible to spend far too much, but a pair of good merino wool socks of the correct size (they're often contoured to fit) are well worth the money.

Also no baggy trousers: they can cause chafing of the inner thighs, which will become an embarrassingly uncomfortable issue, unless you are stick thin or bow legged I suppose. If you have a burning desire to channel MC Hammer while out on the trail, wear some long-legged under shorts beneath your harem pants; you can get the fancy outdoor ones that cost a bomb or buy cheap long johns and cut them down. Trust me, as a man whose inner thighs are no stranger to each other, after 20 odd miles of seemingly harmless swishing, once the chafing sets in, you will do anything to stop your inner thighs from touching – it is deeply uncomfortable. I remember a short exchange, an almost wordless communication I had with a fellow walker, at Beinglas Farm Campsite on day two of my first time on the West Highland Way. I'd covered the best part of forty miles up to that point, not because I am hardy but because I hadn't planned ahead and there had been no safe place to stop. It used to be that, on a weekend, most of Strathclyde would decamp to Loch Lomond for the purpose of getting drunk then collapsing and/or having a fight in a cheap Millets' tent. From Balmaha to the Rowerdennan Lodge, it was essentially seven and a half miles of unbroken drunken disorderliness. I've lived in some excitingly non-gentrified parts of town, but even by my standards, Loch Lomond that evening was just a little bit too tangy. In any case, I'd already walked twenty five miles or thereabouts the previous day from Milngavie to Rowerdennan, then another fourteen miles to Beinglas Farm Campsite that morning in my work socks and some baggy cargo trousers that I think I bought from Tesco. I found myself standing in front of another similarly hobbled and bow-legged walker outside the campsite's amenity block. He took one look at me, nodded and said quietly with compassion and empathy, 'Sudocrem,' then continued on his way.

I should say, they've cracked right down on antisocial camping on Loch Lomond – it's now banned except in designated spots. There are those who say the park authority have gone too far, and to be honest, by banning wild camping over such a wild area, they probably have. Be that as it may, if you find yourself on the banks of Loch Lomond on a weekend night, you'll find they have returned to being quite bonny with little or no chance of being chibbed (a Scots word meaning stabbed…).

Vandalism notwithstanding, I cannot recommend this section of the route highly enough. It was even better with the Fairy Glen but alas, as you read this, it'll be gone. Eleven miles with a handy campsite eight miles or so in, it's ideal for a novice group of young walkers. For us though, the Trailblazer site is somewhat trumped by the British Waterways campsite with its warm toilets and showers, and its proximity to our minibus which contained all our cooking equipment and food (now neatly boxed). After spending a great deal of time skimming stones across Loch Lochy, we packed up and made our way back on to the route proper and to Laggan Locks for our second night under canvas…or nylon anyway…

The shelter at the Trailblazer campsite on Loch Lochy

Dinner this evening for us was a stir fry; I decided not to chance my luck with another meal so recused myself from proceedings. This allowed me to cast an eye over what the young people were eating; on the table were cans of hot dogs, more tomato soup, what looked like a tub of toothpaste but turned out to be a tube filled with the substance found in Milky Ways, and a tub of candy floss. On the bright side, they had succeeded in including some food groups I wasn't even aware existed. Quietly, I asked Lewis to put more stir fry on. On a previous trip along the Great Glen Way while camping at Laggan Locks, leaders had selflessly experimented with food and drink from the barge-cum-pub called The Eagle. It's billed as the only floating pub on the canal, which is mostly true if you discount the two floating hotel/barges that also sell booze on the canal and lochs. Unfortunately, it was closed and going by the sign, when out of season only opened by prior appointment. Since the weather was fine and the temperature nowhere near as cold as it was when we last stayed here, the stir fry was more than adequate and went down very well indeed. The young folk also enjoyed their hotdogs, Milky Way innards and jarred fluff – and the rest of our stir fry. We'd been joined that morning by another member who we'll call Andrew because it's what his parents named him. He was slightly different to other members because he never experienced Cubs or Scouts. His older brother did, but Andrew joined straight in to Explorers at fourteen. It meant that he was new to the group so not familiar with their ways, a notion confirmed by the look on his face when 'dinner' was served that evening. You could say – and you would have a point – that it's our job to show them how to do these things, to teach them if you will. But it's not that they don't know how, it's that they have a hard time making decisions – at least, I think that's what it is. It may also be down to 'The Torture of Choice'; their parents will know what they like so limit options with that knowledge in mind. But in a supermarket with everything laid out before them, they lock up – I know I sometimes do. Often I can be seen corkscrewing in the bread aisle: I'll go in with a clear idea in mind but get distracted by a malt loaf or a 'Best-of-Both', I'll wander from one to the other stuck in a spiral of indecision and before I realise it, find myself rotating slowly on the spot murmuring to myself. I understand the military call it target paralysis – when a soldier or pilot is presented with too many targets, they freeze. I'm like that with ready meals and pies and sausage rolls.

In the end, we had a discussion about it and decided to keep on as we were. The group said if they got really stuck, they'd ask us for some guidance, which seemed like a fair compromise.

The campsite at Laggan Locks is similar to that at Gairlochy: a couple of picnic tables, flat space for tents and the toilets and showers over by. The main difference is there are no fire pits and not much woodland from which to extract fuel. However, in Fort William we'd also picked up some fire logs, handy lumps of compressed wood chip and wood oil. You just light the packaging and it bursts into cheery flames for three hours. Before you light it, it does smell a bit oily, but once burning you can sizzle a sausage with complete peace of mind knowing all the ingredients in the fire log are natural and fully recycled and your banger will taste exactly as it should. While it might not crackle and spark like a proper fire, it brightens the mood and forms a centre piece around which tired walkers and lazy Scouts with sticks can congregate and go over the day's events.

If you need to, because of the site's proximity to the main road, it's a good take out point if you're going to break your trip up. There is a bus stop serviced regularly from Inverness and Fort William and if you don't fancy putting your clothes on back to front, there is a hostel nearby too, pithily named The Great Glen Hostel – we've never stayed there before so you'll have to rely on TripAdvisor for reviews. If you are going to avail yourself of their no doubt stellar services, continue on the Great Glen Way eastward (on the canal towpath) for another mile or so until you come to a small burn known as Allt An Lagain. There, you will find a path up to the main road where you can walk back toward The Great Glen Hostel.

Our second morning dawned as bright as the first. I was first up again wearing a jumper as a pair of trousers and a sock on my head, and as my face slowly regained its normal form and the aches from a second night sleeping on the ground slowly seeped away, I made some coffee and admired the view over Loch Lochy toward Sron a Choire Ghairbh and Meall Na Teanga – the two closest Munros to the route of the Great Glen Way. The former means 'peak of the rough corrie' (a corrie is a large rounded hollow on a hillside often containing a lochan) while the latter means 'man with sock stuck to head'. Of course it doesn't, I'm joking – it means 'round hill of the tongue', which is almost as silly. The day before, the Explorer Scouts had walked along the haunches of both these hills without knowing, and I thought I might suggest going back to bag them, but didn't think they'd be keen. I could tell one or two were not enjoying walking, and I can understand why they might not. When I was a boy (and all of this was open farm land – I've actually said those words entirely without irony), I didn't enjoy hiking either. If you don't have an interest in scenery, not much patience and are used to being wafted from one sensory-satisfying activity to another quickly and comfortably in a parent's car, it's understandable. I know the daily distances weren't much – never more than twelve miles – but if you're not used to it, it can be physically and psychologically challenging. This was my third time on this route with a youth group and my third time not walking with them, so I still didn't know how they were fairing while they walked. I knew from walking the West Highland Way with a group of young people, the first day left them completely shell-shocked, and while some wouldn't talk about it, others were obviously upset about how tough it was turning out to be. But, by the end of day two, they realised that actually, while it *was* tough going, it wasn't going to be impossible – even with full kit. Yesterday when we met the walkers at the campsite at Glas Dhoire they seemed lively enough but by the time we got to the campsite, they had wilted somewhat. This morning as they hobbled back from the shower block for breakfast in a haze of Lynx body spray, they seemed more resigned to the day than looking forward to it.

The route from Laggan Locks to Fort Augustus is flat but the walking is interesting. On canal towpath and forestry roads up until Laggan, it can get a bit samey; however, this part of the route takes in canal towpath, an old railway line and woodland pathways. Even the sections of towpath here offer more of a distraction. Back at Banavie-to-Gairlochy, the canal has a practical industrial feel to it, the waterway meanders on unchanging for six miles but feels like more because as you round one long languorous curve, ahead of you is yet another long, annoyingly languorous curve. The canal is completely uniform in width and you're trapped between it and the River Lochy for the duration. I say trapped, there is one crossing about halfway along at Moy Bridge, you could risk the ire of the farmer and cross the bridge to cut over his land to the minor road that runs between Banavie and Gairlochy. Perhaps being chased by an angry farmer would break the monotony – who knows, he or she might be gruff but avuncular and offer you some yummy eggs and scrumptious cheese. Equally you might get gored by an angry bull – I mean anything could happen really...

The point – which I have somewhat drifted away from – is that the route from Laggan is quite nice. The section from Laggan to the start of Loch Oich on canal towpath is short, then you cross the main road and enter woodland past the Great Glen Water Park – don't get excited, it's a caravan site, there are no flumes. You pick up the old Invergarry and Fort Augustus Railway line for a pleasant loch side amble to Aberchalder where you re-cross the main A82 road and end up back on canal towpath at the swing bridge. This section of canal, although quite long, is still a bit more bearable because it changes, which is to say, the canal doesn't keep its uniform width – sometimes it spreads out a bit and overlaps other water bodies. And there are also two locks: Cullochy and Kytra. I know that sounds incredibly unexciting but things are relative when you're out walking. A thing you'd dismiss as humdrum becomes fascinating because often there's nothing else to hold your attention.

Mentioning Kytra Lock, it was from here on a previous trip we managed to hitch a ride on The Fingal – a large sea-going barge converted into a floating hotel - to Fort Augustus. You may have read about it in the imaginatively named 'The Great Glen Way' (written by the same fair hands bashing this glorious tract out) which describes another trip we took along the route back when Leader Number Three was an Explorer Scout. Kytra is a special place. The A82 is a mile to the south east and there is nothing to the north for many miles, with the only man-made noise coming from boats using the canal or the lock-keeper going about her business and even then, she does that very quietly. It can be busy in the summer as it's within dog walking range of both Fort Augustus and Aberchalder. I've been on the route in April and October (months that book-end the holiday period) and each time there was a steady stream of people passing through. Nevertheless, people seem to understand that, while at Kytra, they are required to observe the silence – it's one of the most restful places I've ever been.

We went about the business of striking camp, with some packing while others fried bacon and poured milk over the picnic table, once done they swapped round. Tents where rolled up but being wet were not put into bags. It's hard enough folding a dry hike tent properly never mind a wet one, and often it seems they're designed not to be repacked into whatever bag they came in. We'd be laying the tents out to dry later that day anyway and wouldn't need them that night because we were going to be staying in microcabins on the banks of

Loch Ness near Invermoriston. With the litter sweep done and all the cooking gear packed away, Michael, who'd be walking with the group today, put one of the two-way radios in his pocket and prepared to leave. Before they set off though, one of the young people approached me tentatively. I like to think I'm a congenial sort so wondered why he was being so hesitant – he reached up, removed the sock still stuck to my head and handed it to me with a look of gentle concern.

Say what you like about the youth of today – they're not all bad.

Day Three – Laggan Locks to Fort Augustus

Looking south west from the north shore of Loch Lochy near to Laggan Lock

While the main group walked toward Fort Augustus, Lewis and I drove. We thought it would be good fun to hire a canoe or boat and paddle back along the canal to meet the group, but turns out you can't – there are no boats, canoes, rubber rings or anything else remotely buoyant available to hire in October between Invergarry and Invermoriston. So we did some shopping instead, picking up some essentials we were missing. The group would need to buy breakfast for the following morning, but since we'd be travelling through Inverness the following afternoon, we would shop for the next two or three days there. We'd done a fair bit of gadding about looking for boats or canoes and it was close to lunchtime, so Lewis and I decided to procure a bowl of soup and a hot chocolate from MacVeans Supermarket & Café – sorry – I meant Restaurant. I'm not sure what properties an establishment must display in order to obtain restaurant status because, to me, MacVeans is a café. I don't want to sound like a snob, but if you have to push a tray along a shelf in front of glass cases containing cakes and sandwiches which you pay for before you eat, that is a café. But since we might be buying breakfast goods from the attached 'Supermarket', we didn't make a scene. There is another shop round the corner from MacVeans which is usually better stocked if you don't mind petrol station prices. It also sells things like gas canisters and other assorted camping accoutrement, which is handy. Attached to it is an eye-wateringly expensive gift shop, supported by the large coach and car park nearby. Even in October it's busy, two or three coach parties from different parts of the world shuffling around snapping pictures and holding bags bulging with expensive tourist tat. I love foreign tourists; their unalloyed curiosity is refreshing, and they seem to be so much happier than people visiting from other parts of the UK. I suppose it's easy to work out why: someone from Bromley will know that paying double figures for a tin of shortbread is a bit of an affront and while they might otherwise quite like the porcelain Scottie Dog (hand-painted by a local artist), the exorbitant price tag has them reaching for their inhalers. Not so with the Japanese; they're either smiling or confused – but either way they seem to be happy. The only Japanese tourists who aren't happy are the children.

I'm not sure what words adequately describe Japanese youth fashion – cartoon chic, perhaps? Whichever it is, they do like to make an effort: skinny jeans, training shoes with over-sized tongues or minimalist plimsolls, expensive looking elaborately designed jackets with huge lapels worn over T shirts sporting trendy motifs. Unlike their parents though, their faces are tripping them – they couldn't be more miserable – and who can blame them, stuck on a coach with mum and dad, granny and granddad and assorted siblings for a fortnight. Still, it ruins the ambience – they could at least buy a locally manufactured cashmere snood and use it to hide their disdain. Other tourists were mostly Spanish who are suspicious of everything, which I suppose is not surprising. They're visiting a country that exports large numbers of knobs and hooligans to Spanish nightclubs – during the peak months they paint Spanish avenues and alleyways with vomit. In some respects, for a Spaniard visiting the UK, it must be a bit like visiting a zoo where many of the enclosures have been left open – I can understand why they're on their guard.

Anyway, Lewis and I finished our soup and hot chocolate and made to leave. As we stepped outside onto the pavement, a handsome Italian couple wafted by in a cloud of expensive perfume peddling rented electric bikes. We looked at each other and had the same thought, 'It's not a canoe, but it's something different. Let's investigate.' We plodded up the road and found a lady sitting in a van with some electric bikes on side stands. I plucked a leaflet from a rack and read the blurb: for £24 each we could have a bike for the afternoon. We agreed, left a deposit and went back to the minibus to pick up backpacks and supplies.

The lady said that as we pedalled, the bike would know and apply power to an electric motor driving the back wheel. The harder we peddled the more power it would supply, although it was limited to 24kph. Given the time – about 2pm – we thought the walkers would be about to cross the road at Aberchalder swing bridge, which was five miles from Fort Augustus. At 24kph, we could be there in, ummm, hold on now… five miles is about, ooooh, let me see… erm, eight kilometres? At 24kph that meant…oh my, this is difficult…three hours? That didn't sound right at all. If we averaged 16kph it would take, what, half an hour? It didn't really matter as we'd meet them at some point because there's not much scope to get lost. I hadn't ridden a bike for a while, at least not one with pedals, but I threw my leg over the saddle and set off. The immediate question was: why hadn't I tried this before? It was great, you pedalled quite gently and the electric motor would whirr quietly away just like the lady described. It was like a gentle shove from behind. The canal towpath is mostly flat with only a few gentle undulations, so once we'd built up speed it was easy to maintain it. Unfortunately, the canal towpath is far from smooth. Indeed it is as far from smooth as I am from competing in the Tour de France. These bikes are known in the trade as 'hardtails' because, bewilderingly, only the front forks have suspension, which would have been great if that's where you were sitting. The rear had no such cushioning: it was basically a thin saddle, a metal post and thin bit of rubber filled to bursting with air then the unforgiving ground. It was impossible to sit down while moving so we hovered and pedalled, then pedalled and hovered until we got to Kytra where we stopped for a moment to recover.

I don't wish to sound indelicate, but we felt by the time we got to the walkers we'd both be split roughly up the middle. As it turned out, we got to the swing bridge at Aberchalder well in advance of the group with bodies bruised but intact. The plan was to let the group pass us then cycle up from behind and pedal majestically and effortlessly past.

I was genuinely miffed to be missing this part of the route, as it's a really nice walk along the banks of Loch Oich. Once you come off the canal towpath and cross the main road into the Great Glen Water Park, the route takes on a different tone altogether. Passed the wooden chalets of the water park you join the old railway line and everything becomes verdant and peaceful. It's been a number of years since I walked this part of the route, but I don't imagine anything has changed too much, it's not forestry plantation land so the trees (mostly deciduous) should remain as they are with only nature looking in on them. The path bypasses some old train tunnels that at the time I didn't venture into and at times dips down to the lochside.

About a mile past the last of the water park's chalets, if you look through the trees to the other side of the loch, you might be able to see the monument marking the Well of the Seven Heads. A gruesome story remembered by an obelisk, which is itself quite grisly – a trim ashlar pyramid on a square base, topped with seven severed heads held by a hand also holding a dagger (they must have had big hands back then). This stuff is priceless if you have kids with you, especially if you're camping. Ours are a bit old for ghost stories, but if you've got pre-teens, you can really scare the crap out of them – not that I advocate such irresponsible behaviour.

In any case, purely for information, dependent on source, seven severed heads were washed either in a spring situated beneath the obelisk or in the loch's water nearby. Previously, the heads used to belong to Alexander MacDonald of Inverlair (a place near Roy Bridge) and his six sons. On the 26th September 1663, they'd argued with and killed a fellow called Alexander MacDonald of Keppoch and his brother Ranald, both of whom had recently returned from France. At the time the two Keppoch MacDonald's were not well liked. They were seen as a bit hoity-toity and so, because of that, their despatch went largely unremarked. However, another MacDonald called Ian Lom aka Bald Iain – another Keppoch MacDonald - decided he'd avenge their murder. Scottish clans not only argued and fought with each other, they argued and fought internally, which makes it quite difficult to explain given many of the men had the same first and second names. I suppose I could just say the two Keppoch MacDonalds were killed by seven Inverlair MacDonalds. Bald Iain MacDonald was so pissed off he embarked upon a crusade for vengeance, -which he duly got after persuading Sir James MacDonald of Sleat (who knew the Keppoch men slightly) to request from the Privy Council in Edinburgh a letter of 'fire and sword' against the killers. This they duly did and Sir James sent his brother Archibald – a warrior poet, no less – with fifty men, guided by Bald Iain, to murder and decapitate Alexander MacDonald of Inverlair and his six sons and very likely a number of others besides.

Once the deed was done, Bald Iain gathered up the heads and wrapped them in plaid – even back then, it was the little things. He tied the grisly package off with willow in anticipation of the journey to Invergarry Castle where he planned to show them to the High Chief of Clan Donald, Lord MacDonnell of Glengarry – lucky him. At some point, he decided that the severed heads were in a far from presentable condition so stopped to rinse them in the water of Loch Oich where the obelisk stands today.

It's a 17th century version of The Jeremy Kyle Show, we probably shouldn't judge…

Iain Lom MacDonald was one of the first Gaelic poet laureates – long before Robert Burns had the role – who wrote about the 1707 Treaty of Union, the Hanoverian succession and the Glen Coe Massacre. He also wrote about the Keppoch Murders although it's not known if he included the bit where he washed seven severed heads in the waters of Loch Oich. He was known as Bald Iain not necessarily because he was follically challenged but because he was a plain talker. He was well known but perhaps not well liked for his quick and vitriolic tongue, possibly to compensate for being somewhat disabled – he was described at the time as 'walking with a hirple' or a limp in today's language. The Trailblazer campsite at Leiterfearn is a good bit past the monument, so if you do have kids with you, you'll need to set them up in advance – being followed in the woods by seven shambling headless bodies (even during the day) is going to set them on edge. If you have transport, it's worth visiting the monument. It was possible to go down to the lochside behind the monument and enter the narrow tunnel to where the spring gurgled from the rock, although it is entirely possible that it has been blocked off for reasons of health and safety. Assuming it is accessible, I recommend going at night but, in advance of your visit, placing seven crudely carved turnips in the tunnel. Before you send the kids in, say something like, 'Wouldn't it be a scream to go in with the torches switched off? Yeah, let's do that…' Henceforth, the monument might be known as the Well of the Seven Years under strict social work supervision. Well, it adds a bit of tang to the family holiday.

There is an alternative Great Glen Way route on the north side of Loch Oich. I haven't walked it myself, but it's described as being 'more varied in terms of path surface and gradient'. Although it doesn't visit the lochside, it does pass through Invergarry which means shops, pubs and hotels.

But getting back on track … it was easy to see how Lewis and I got to the swing bridge before the walkers did, given the pace they'd adopted for the day, they were obviously not being chased by any undead headless highlanders. We didn't really mind because the distances were more than manageable – they had time to doddle. Also, I well remember as a young Scout being harangued for not walking at a pace which pleased my elders. I was one of those children who could always be found at the coo's tail as we still like to say in Scotland. I'd be plodding along in wellies that were far too big or far too small while some nasty Venture Scout or some nameless leader told me how crap I was at walking. I would reply with something pithy like, 'The only reason you manage to walk so well is by concentrating hard. I can see the strain in your face.' At which point it was necessary to break into a run, which wellies are not designed for, at least not in 1984 they weren't. On one such night hike – known to non-Scouting types as 'walking in the dark' – we managed to convince a fellow Scout the honking noise we could all hear was the call of the haggis. We told him they looked a bit like sheep and ate small pebbles, so he duly filled the large front pocket of his orange cagoule with smooth flat pebbles. Whenever he heard a honk, he'd lob a pebble into the darkness. We also told him they were able to extend or retract their legs dependant on what way they were walking round the hillside, though by then I think we'd lost him. I have a nostalgic snapshot in my mind of him pulling pebbles out of that big orange pocket and dumping them on the ground with good-natured frustration. It was all nonsense, of course, because we were walking near Megget Water which is in the Scottish Borders, and everyone knows haggis are not native to the Scottish Borders.

But I've digressed again, which is as well because our youths were moving at a glacial speed. Eventually we watched them appear from the woods on Loch Oich's southern shores, then across the A82 and the Aberchalder Swing Bridge and continue on the towpath to Cullochy Locks in the near distance, which was our cue to throw legs over saddles and freewheel down from our vantage point back onto the canal towpath. We caught up with the group, forcing them to leap off the path as we clattered uncomfortably past (I still think a canoe would have been more fun, and better for the fillings in my teeth). Michael insisted on having a shot on one of the bikes, we all watched him zip up and down the towpath until we got bored and pushed a stick through the front wheel. I'm joking, we didn't do that at all. We'd brought some juice and snacks in a backpack for the group so we shared it all out while Leader Number Three gingerly disentangled himself from the wreckage of the bike. I remember Michael saying he was a keen cyclist, he once said he wanted to tour Scotland on a bicycle, he used to talk about designer panniers and all sorts of other cycling paraphernalia, although all that may have changed since he passed his driving test. If he still intended to embark upon such a journey, an electric bike would be great – especially for the hilly bits.

I think by this time the young people where looking forward to being finished the walking section of the trip. Some might say they hadn't walked far, but relatively speaking, they'd done quite well. While it's true some were in the midst of doing Duke of Edinburgh awards, none were at gold level where even then, specific distances are not stipulated. At bronze level, expedition requirements are two days/one night with a six-hour day of which three hours must be spent moving, although it doesn't say at what speed. Silver level is three days/two nights with a seven-hour day of which three and half hours must be spent in an ambulant fashion. Our trip was supposed to be enjoyable, and I've never understood masochistic holidays, I mean, why would you? I understand people wishing to challenge themselves and deriving a sense of satisfaction out of it – but that wasn't the point of this trip. I'm still not sure what the point of it was if I'm being honest … something to do with scenery, I think … I don't really remember.

As we all set off again, crossing the canal at Cullochy Locks as a group, I realised this was only the second time we'd all travelled together not sitting in the minibus. While we man-handled the bikes along the narrow lock gates and onto the grass, the lock-keeper came out and gave us a row for cycling on the grass. Since Lewis and I had done no such thing, the kids – loyal to a fault - became incensed at the injustice and threw him into the canal. Of course they didn't, I made that up. We moved the bikes (which we'd put on the grass with side-stands deployed) onto the path and set off ahead of the group – the bikes were due back and we had strict instructions not to be late.

I wish I could say more about what the young folk got up to and the conversations or thoughts they had while they walked. The truth is, up until Fort Augustus, I saw very little of them during the day. All I had to go on was what Lewis said about the first day from Gairlochy to Laggan Locks and what Michael said of the second day from Laggan Locks to Fort Augustus. I did ask Lewis, but he shrugged his shoulders and said he didn't understand much of what they talked about, and while Michael could make out a lot of the things they said, he wasn't able to communicate it in a way Lewis and I could understand. From what I can gather, there was talk of Doctor Who (which I don't watch), chat about elves and goblins (about whom I know nothing having never seen the right films), much quoting of Monty Python (eminently quotable stuff, but only funny when Monty Python do it – sorry, it's true), and in-depth analysis of the back catalogue of The Beatles. Over the week we came to this conclusion: the young people seemed to have perfect recall and were seemingly able to hold long conversations using quotes from popular TV shows and You Tube clips – to what end, I have no idea. We felt sure if they were on a plane and the flight crew had been sucked out the windows, they'd be able to memorise the flight manual word for word but wouldn't be able to land the plane.

Perhaps it's just the way of things, maybe it's me and not them – in fact, it probably is. All they're doing is using social references to which they can relate to communicate ideas. That I can't relate to them isn't their fault, it's mine for not wanting to sit through hours of turgid indecipherable films about goblins, orks or wizards. It also explains why they just stand and stare when I'm explaining some very simple concepts using Gregorian chants.

It was also becoming apparent the group dynamic was different to previous generations of Explorer Scouts; this group didn't really want to spend time with leaders. I've been involved in youth work in all sorts of contexts; I've managed a youth café delivering social education and smoothies, and worked for the Department of Social Work in some challenging circumstances. Each setting has its own parameters, boundaries that develop organically as time passes, along with those that are deliberately put in place for practical operational reasons. Our Scout Group is quite laid back, more so with the older sections. Explorer Leaders don't wear uniforms for example and we don't insist Explorers do. It's deliberate on our part, at age 14 or 15, they're very much moving from childhood into adulthood and we try to reflect that in how we treat them. We try as much as possible to treat them as peers. No more spoon-fed instructions, we explain what we need to do and furnish them with all the information. We don't say do it this way or that, we say these are your options, what would you like to do? Our previous batch of young people, now mostly left for university or work – of which

Michael was a part – took full advantage of this. We would sit together at dinner or round a campfire and the discussion seemed to find equilibrium between the age ranges present. With this new intake, that wasn't happening. There was the odd exception – Andrew for example, plus one or two others took advantage of the wider latitude being treated as an adult offers. I mean they weren't drinking Prosecco or injecting heroin between their toes, but they would just sit up a bit later and take part in the discussion which might have been about anything from organisational stuff to the new warning light that had appeared in the minibus, or to wonder if the Land Rover I bought was lonely sitting on its own at home.

Perhaps among young people there is an assumption that when adults are chatting, it is about lofty considerations beyond the ken of young minds – I was going to suggest that it might sometimes be the case, but genuinely, I can't think why leaders wouldn't want all the input they could get. Equally, young folk might not think grown ups want them to sit around during so called adult talk. With us, it's not the case, you'd only need to sit for a few minutes to understand that the talk isn't particularly grown up. Brace yourselves, I'm going to be serious for a moment. Adults who volunteer to work with young people do so for many different reasons, from the downright nefarious to the most enlightened motives. Some do it for the simple satisfaction of a hobby, others because it gives them something to moan about and others still do it purely so they can rub their charitable work in people's faces. The following statement may shock some people, but volunteering to work with young people is more often than not quite selfish. Let me explain. We volunteer because it's great fun. You know all the things we wanted to do as kids such as go-karting, abseiling, gorge-walking, fire-lighting, camping, and much more besides, but rarely did because no one could take us or we didn't have the money? We do all that stuff. All those childish pursuits we grudgingly put away when we become adults and are now too self-conscious to try even though we have the resources to do it? We do all that stuff, too. Not only do you get to do it, you get to do it with people not yet encumbered by adult inhibitions that so often develop, people who are uniquely placed to enjoy it in a way that is often lost to grown ups – kids. So you see, it really is an incredibly selfish pursuit.

Every now and again, there will be a boy or girl who will come along and your efforts will be the making of them – you might never know it was, or the how or why of it, you may even save their life in some incredibly subtle and incidentally far-sighted way and never know until a parent mentions it months or years later. It might not happen often, but it will happen. That it does is an excellent side effect of your selfish volunteering ways.

Fort Augustus is an attractive settlement; the town's centre piece must be the canal locks which raises (or lowers) canal traffic between Loch Ness and the canal to Kytra Lock. (Heading westward, Kytra raises the level again to Cullochy Lock which in turn raises the level of the canal to Loch Oich and its highest elevation of 32 metres above sea level). The town buzzes with tourists in the high season but is busy all year round with coach parties. As we returned our electric bikes to the lady and her van halfway down the locks, a crowd of people had gathered to watch a surprisingly large and new-looking boat make its way upwards. As you would imagine, it's a slow process. The boat is tied off as water levels equalise, the lock gates swing open and the boat is untied so it can edge slowly forward to a place where it is secured again – all of which is repeated five times. I don't wish to appear cynical, but once people realised the skipper wasn't going to prang the obviously brand new boat off a wall or canal fixing, they soon began to disperse. Lewis and I, with time to kill, followed the shiny orange boat's progress, and eventually it emerged unscathed from the top lock and moored up for the night. Shortly thereafter our group of intrepid if very slow Explorers appeared by the locks looking as if they'd had enough of walking for the day, which was fortunate because as far as walking was concerned, they were finished. From this point on, we'd be covering around 150 miles a day in the minibus – assuming no new lights appeared on the dashboard which might cause it to implode.

Dinner was next on the agenda. Adults with money are generously catered for by the many pubs and restaurants in the area, but if you are on a budget, there is a chip shop at the top of the locks and at the bottom where the canal merges with Loch Ness, a takeaway establishment. The chip shop from the outside doesn't look promising but it's actually very good – it's also one of very few chip shops I've seen that sells red pudding. I have no idea what red pudding is – I know what black pudding is and I've seen white pudding (although it does reminds me of those desiccated dog poos I used to see when I was a child). So I will admit to a certain amount of trepidation and hesitance, which coming from someone who enjoys black pudding (a foodstuff which may include anything), readers will be forgiven for not understanding. It just looks a bit suspect, which is possibly down to the colour. The ingredients of a red pudding on the surface seem acceptable: pork, bacon, pork rind, beef, suet, wheat flower, beef fat, spices, salt and rusks (presumably not the type fed to toddlers.). Black pudding contains blood from a pig, oatmeal and onions plus pork fat among other things. A white pudding on the other hand contains oatmeal, beef suet, onions, spices and generous amounts of Dulux Pure Brilliant White matt emulsion. I'm joking, it doesn't have paint in it at all, white pudding doesn't contain blood, which explains its pale complexion. If you find yourself at this chip shop, I'd recommend the fish – the proprietor cooks everything from scratch and its well worth the wait.

The takeaway at the bottom of the locks – known as The Moorings – occupies a prime spot, which is a shame because it's a bit shit. Four or five of us wandered down for some takeaway pizza but across all of our transactions and some others that took place as we waited, the man serving didn't say a word beyond angrily mumbled requests for payment. It's been a long while since I worked in the hospitality trade and I wouldn't claim to have been a ray of sunshine at the time, but it was difficult to know if this fellow wanted to kill us or kill himself. A quick search on TripAdvisor paints a similar picture. Personally, assuming you're not going to be poisoned or harmed in any real sense, I think these establishments add a certain tang to a trip – it gives you something to laugh about later on. I'm not saying going out for something to eat and everything about it being lovely is unacceptable, it's just that sometimes turning up at a place that is so crap it's funny, can be hugely entertaining. The pizzas when they eventually arrived were fine, and no one ended up hurling into the canal so really, as long as you don't mind being glared at by a furiously glum-looking waiter, all's well that ends well.

If you're doing all of the Great Glen Way, Fort Augustus is the halfway point and a good place to stock up on food. The shop at the garage has a limited range of camping equipment, and crucially, if you need to stock up on gas, when we were there they had a decent range of brands. If you want to have a night indoors, there are B&Bs and a big hostel called Stravaigers Lodge, which we've never actually seen open. There is no designated British Waterways campsite at Fort Augustus, which I've always felt is a bit cynical. I'm all for supporting local business but when the only budget accommodation option is closed for half the year, it's annoying. I should say though, there is a Trailblazer site at Kytra Lock about three miles short of the town – but it does mean you miss out on great fish and chips, takeaway pizza and angry glares from sullen waiters.

In the past we've always travelled on to the Hobbit microcabins at the Loch Ness Holiday Park. These for us represent the best value for money, working out at less than £15 per head per night, and the setting is about as nice as can be with views across Loch Ness. If you don't see the monster from here, you'll probably never see it.

There is a large hotel in Fort Augustus if you're feeling flush, called The Lovat, named after the local landowners. It's quite swish. I fell through their doors on my first foray along the Great Glen Way, and I was at that stage where I was prepared to pay significant sums of money for the most meagre comforts. The first thing to make me suspicious of the tariff was being piped in the door by a man in full highland regalia. I remember thinking if this was the standard, booking in wasn't going to be cheap. The piper wasn't for me though; I was disturbing someone's nuptials. At least the skirl of the pipes masked the instinctive yelp I give when the receptionist told me how much a single room was. I hobbled away to a B&B down the road a bit, cursing gently as I went.

There are always moments recalled with particular gladness from trips and holidays. All of us sitting halfway down the locks eating dinner is one of them – we chatted away about this and that while water cascaded noisily over the lock gates. Lewis and I hadn't done anything like the same amount of walking as the main group had that day, but we were all in good spirits. With the walking phase of the trip done, we were about to embark upon a bit of an adventure. Only one or two of our group had travelled north of Inverness, and as this was also our last night with planned accommodation, from here on, it was going to be, as I said, a bit of an adventure.

With dinner eaten, we decided that instead of buying breakfast for the following day, and since we were travelling in a minibus with another Scout group's name emblazoned on its sides, we'd just ram-raid the garage. Oh dear, there I go again, we didn't do that at all – the youngsters decided what to have and bought it fair and square. However, our solitary vegetarian was forgotten again, although no one would imagine he'd be standing the following morning eating cornflakes with brown sauce on a roll. I mean, we had milk, spoons and bowls – looking back, it was probably a cry for help. As we returned to the van with our victuals, we noticed another fault had developed. The side door hadn't been locking when we pressed the button on the fob, but it was impossible to know for how long this had been happening because we hadn't been checking. There was no keyhole on the outside and no knob to press on the inside. Eventually we worked it out, although I don't remember exactly how, but we managed to get the door to lock – it might have involved the smallest Explorer climbing out of a window, but we got there.

Hobbit microcabins are great fun and cheap to rent, and they come in different set ups – some sleep four or six and some sleep two. The cabins on Loch Ness slept four – two singles and a double. It meant some of the young people would have to sleep top to toe but given they'd been camping the previous two nights in pokey hike tents, it was still a step up. We picked up our keys and carried on – to the horror of several people peering out from their camper vans – to our cabins. Scouts get a mixed response from the public. I remember years ago during a summer camp going to church on the Sunday morning – it's something we used to do. We'd take the kids to the nearest Church of Scotland service, regardless of their faith (we're more mindful now), where they'd sit and fidget and giggle for the duration – even the leaders were bored. On this occasion it was a sizeable church in a small place called Greenlaw in the Scottish Borders. Unfortunately, the tiny congregation was somewhat lost in the large square footage, our presence had increased that morning's attendance to the extent that the minister nearly cracked a smile. He started off as ministers do and we soon arrived at the first hymn. Picture the scene: an old but well kept church, a diminished but still proud – and devout – congregation, an old but enthusiastic minister, possibly close to a contented retirement in the parish he served so loyally. One Sunday morning, the usual small crowd shuffles in with no expectation of anything other than their normal weekly commune with God. But no, today would be different. God in his beneficence had sent a Boy Scout troop – oh the joy, finally youth is returned, these dusty pews will know the sweet song of childhood. Okay, they looked a bit scruffy, but they were in uniform: neckers were straight with woggles in place. The minister announces the hymn number, the organ bursts into sonorous voice, after the intro we all stand and at the same time several geriatric necks creak in anticipation as they look up to the balcony where the minister put us. The expectation is palpable, these people are expecting the pure voice of youth, they're expecting a choir – what they got was a noise similar to that which would be made some years later by my pal Sheridan, scaring an angry stag with a traffic cone in a hotel car park.

The disappointment was tangible and acutely embarrassing; the expectation was to become closer to the Lord Jesus through the medium of mellifluous song – what they got was tinnitus.

Others look upon all young people with suspicion whether they're part of a youth organisation or not. They see a group of youths and immediately clutch handbags, small children and pets to their bosom in anticipation of being mugged – which for us would have been fine because they'd assume we were from Fife.

The truth, for us anyway, is while in the past we've had members who have gone off the rails, the young folk with us that week were (and continue to be) thoroughly decent individuals. If they were accused of some wrongdoing or other, I'd look at their accuser and wonder if they were on drugs. In the past we've applied for grants from programs and trusts whose main objective is to fund 'distraction' activities – the idea being to divert the attentions of young people away from more nefarious pursuits toward more wholesome activities such as gorge walking or rock climbing. I genuinely can't imagine any of this current crowd getting into trouble; they're all far too nice. We've been successful in getting funding from these sources in the past, and while we've been a bit gallus in accepting it on the grounds that it would keep our members from a sure life of crime, we still don't have the brass neck to do guaranteed money spinners like bag packs, or sponsored events we'd probably enjoy doing anyway. At Scouts, we are asked quite often to support school-based activities – specifically the eye-wateringly expensive foreign trips that are so fashionable these days. We've had members go to Ecuador, Borneo and Malawi to name but a few and each time these trips come round, so do the requests for cash donations. Now I don't begrudge them their trip – not for a minute – but I'm not going to help pay for it, partly because it's a bit of a holiday and because I'm miserable in a more general sense. Okay, they might build a few metres of path in forests or put together some flat pack school desks, but time and again they come back from these life-changing trips and apologetically tell us it was a bit of a jolly after all. Also, they're away for almost a month, half spent in cheap hostels and the other half in tents, and it still cost close to £4k. If I was a parent my kids would be miserable. If organisers were a bit more honest about it and just took them on a round the world cruise or something, at least it would be better value for money – I might even go with them.

We settled into our cabins: Michael, Lewis and I in one while the Explorer Scouts arm wrestled over who'd get to have Rhianna in their cabin – I'm joking, that didn't happen. When Scouts became mixed, it was a provocative decision, not least for the other similar youth organisation that still only caters for girls. Leaders were up in arms about how awkward it could be, while others thought the influx in membership would only be good. We were quite late in taking girls on, not because we had an issue with it but because the village where we operate has a well organised Guide group. Now though, while we're nowhere near parity, we have a number of girls across all the sections, and so far, no awkwardness or unintended consequences have occurred. We thought having girls aboard would temper the wilder behaviour of the boys but to be honest, we've not noticed much of a change. If anything, the girls who do join are accepted as being 'one of the boys'. This is certainly true for Explorers – Rhianna is always outnumbered but holds her own and gets stuck in with the rest of them. I'm not sure what the detractors thought might happen with Scouts being mixed, but whatever it was, it hasn't occurred because it's all been quite unexceptional from our point of view.

I did have an interesting conversation with one of our Scouts (a boy) during our first summer camp with a girl in attendance. He said he didn't think it was fair that girls could join Scouts but boys couldn't join Guides. I said, wouldn't be folly for a boy to even want to join Guides, I mean, wouldn't he'd get it in the neck from his pals? His reply was enlightening and from my point of view slightly embarrassing because it highlighted a flaw in my reasoning. He saw no such issues around a boy wanting to join Guides, all he saw was an imbalance; girls were now attending Scouts but boys were still not allowed to join Guides. I had blithely formed an opinion based on a negative stigma and in doing so, propagated what is in reality a bit of a blot on our society. Where he was all about fairness, I'd fallen back on outdated preconceptions. That a lad might be bullied for expressing a wish to join Guides is not a reason to dismiss the idea – instead we should be challenging (energetically) the attitudes of knuckle draggers who'd be doing the bullying, because that is where the problem truly lies.

He went on to say he felt Scouts was no longer a place where boys could be boys, and at the time I thought he might be right (without really knowing exactly what he meant). Eventually he left the organisation, which was a shame because looking back it hasn't changed the tone very much at all. It's just as irreverent and the boys are just as faux macho as they ever were. I suppose the main difference is there are now girls around to be thoroughly unimpressed by it. That said, any ten-year-old (boy or girl) who joins Scouts will be no shrinking violet when it comes to certain hardships. While we try to cater for all, it's still a rough and tumble organisation. Members will at some point be expected to go more than a day or two without a bath, and activities are often hands-on so can become rough – although not overly so, we do try to limit injury where possible.

The point is, it turns out it's not about boys and girls, it's about people. Some young folk relish the thought of poking a fire with a stick or sleeping under a hedge, while others do not. Some youngsters can tolerate an evening with an unknown number of spiders, moths or Daddy-Long-Legs in their tent – others, not so much so. Are there boys who don't join Scouts because it's mixed? Maybe. Have there been boys who left because it became mixed? Unfortunately, yes. In an organisation where attendance is voluntary, membership tends to suit the prevailing conditions – and that's where we're at just now with Scouts.

Either way, the Explorer Scouts most assuredly did not arm wrestle over who got to sleep where. I dare say, had it even been suggested, a dead arm or a withering stare from Rhianna would have put that person in their place. There is only so much bravado a male – whatever their age – can get away with around girls, even with superior numbers.

As leaders sat up around the picnic tables outside our cabins, we watched Explorers go to the shower block clutching toilet bags and towels to return two hours later wearing night gowns and caps. Some went straight to their microcabins to play cards or chat; others sat up with leaders to chat and eat Doritos and biscuits. This was the quality time. As a group we'd replay and rehash the day's events. It's always entertaining, and reliving events was useful for those of us who hadn't been with the main group that day. It also helps to further embed for the record memories of the trip.

Lewis and I had spent very little time that day with the group while Leader Number Three, our missing link and occasional interpreter, had seen and heard it all first-hand. We were fast coming to realise that no matter how much we tried to understand the social references the young folk were using, they would forever be objects in a dimly lit room to us. I think Lewis knew more than he let on but was feigning ignorance to spare my feelings. Leader Number Three – or Michael as his parents sometimes call him – on the other hand was revelling in his new found relevance. Every now and again he'd glance with disdain at the glazed look on my face – I'd claim to be scanning the dark waters of Loch Ness for signs of the monster but he'd just laugh cruelly. Of course, I'm joking, the Explorers sitting munching on crisps and biscuits had managed to dumb down the chat to accommodate my tenuous grasp of current social trends. Once they'd accepted I hadn't seen anything of something called 'The Inbetweeners', manifold films about wizards, goblins and hobbits, COD (which is nothing to do with fish) and much more besides, they adjusted their conversational input accordingly. Instead, once we'd exhausted chat about what we'd done that day and would be doing the next, we talked about The Antiques Road Show and Coronation Street while I passed round the Werther's Originals.

Day Four – Invermoriston to Thurso

Microcabins on Loch Ness. They're all gone now, replaced by posh cabins – a real shame

One hundred and sixty six miles. I know, a bit of a change of pace for the fourth day, but at least we'd be well rested after a comfortable night in our microcabins. Seniority brings certain perks – as it should – so I had the double sleeping platform with its plastic covered piece of foam to myself. It was situated furthest from the door beneath a small window, while the two single beds occupied by Leaders Number Two and Three ran down either side of the cabin toward some storage, a small fridge and a fan heater attached to the wall. We'd stayed in these microcabins before so knew they could become a bit airless, and by airless I mean smelly – the small windows really needed to be open if in the morning you wanted to draw a conscious breath that wouldn't make you gag.

Taking advantage of the space no one would be using on my deluxe sleeping platform, I carried out an inventory before going to sleep. I upended my rucksack and methodically laid out all that it contained so I knew exactly what I had, what I'd lost or what I'd perhaps gained. We used to do this regularly on summer camps, spending a week in such close proximity to others roughly your own size meant by the end of the week you probably wouldn't be wearing any of your own clothes. Items of clothing would migrate from one end of the tent to the other, while other people's socks would be found at the bottom of sleeping bags weeks after the camp had finished. As a kid, it was a pain; as a leader, it was something of a necessity in order to assuage complaints from parents who could be forgiven for thinking their kid had come home with the wrong bag. In the days and weeks after camp, sad little totes of unclaimed belongings would appear here and there and then perhaps disappear from the Scout Hall as items slowly filtered back to their rightful owners. Often though, these lonely reminders of camp would end up in the wheelie bin.

Full kit inspection – as it is known – meant picking a morning (when it wasn't raining), to pull the ground sheet out of your patrol tent and set out all your belongings on your sleeping bag. Younger scouts would arrange clothes in the shape of a person while older scouts would fold theirs. Shoes and socks would go at the bottom then trousers, T-shirts and jumpers, and so on, up to the top. 'Smalls' could be presented for inspection or kept demurely to one side (now that Scouts is a mixed organisation I assume the Scout section follow the latter course). The main purpose of the exercise was to make sure everybody got their belongings back, to air the patrol tent and to confiscate any truly offensive weapons or printed materiel; but it was also an opportunity to confirm whether or not the children had been cleaning behind their ears. This was often a problem at camp – we'd open soap boxes and peer accusingly at dry soap untouched by moisture and at still-sealed tubes of toothpaste as the child stood looking sheepish and grubby.

Now-a-days the opposite is true. Sure enough, you still get the groans of protest as full kit inspections are announced with clothes being laid out as before, stray socks tracked down and sweets thought long consumed discovered squashed flat beneath sleeping mats. However, toilet bags are quite a different matter. They no longer contain soap; it's all moisturising body wash (because soap dries the skin obviously) and hair gel abounds along with exfoliating body scrubs and vitamin D enriched facial pads. To be fair, the crowd we had away on this trip had no such pretensions, except perhaps for an over-use of deodorant. Some of the group that came through Scouts with Leader Number Three had very high standards indeed, resulting in us frequently being late for activities because someone was putting Hot Fudge Holding Gel in their hair or taking care of their T-zone – whatever that means.

At some point during the night, I must have had a seizure because the items I had so neatly laid out to one side the night before were now spread over and around where I lay. Leaders Number Two and Three seemed still to be sleeping so I threw shoes at them until they woke up – I'm joking, I didn't do that, it would have been silly. Instead, I disentangled myself from the belongings I'd so neatly sorted through the night before and exited my bariatric sleeping bag which, going by the mess, had indeed afforded me more room to move about.

Michael and Lewis stirred as I opened the doors to a bright Tuesday morning. Loch Ness coruscated cheerily under the sunlight and anyone who happened to be looking would have seen the long languorous curve of the Loch Ness Monster's muscular body as it gently broke the water's surface some way off. I suppose it could have been a log because my eyes weren't quite right. Gently rubbing the eye bogies (it's what we called 'sleep' in our house) from the corners of my eyes, I looked again at the shimmering waters of the loch – yup, just a log.

Explorers from one cabin were up and showered, but the occupants of the other seemed still to be asleep. Flinging the doors open was, in hindsight, a bit foolhardy – the smell that assaulted the senses was tangible. Once my eyes stopped watering, I could see through the miasma that the small window at the far end of the cabin was still closed. I was about to dive in and start checking for pulses but one after the other of the four sleeping forms began to move. Bleary eyes peered from inside sleeping bags as the last of the fug escaped out into the atmosphere. I said we'd be starting breakfast imminently and they should probably think about packing up. I had no idea who was in this cabin, and paying too much attention to young people as they lie in their sleeping bags is a sure fire way to get on a register, so these days we count the shapeless bumps and hope for the best.

In the meantime, those of us who were up spread out the still damp tents we'd forgotten to dry the previous day and started on breakfast. As before, we lit Trangias and other stoves to fry bacon and square sausage. While that went on, rough-looking Explorers slopped milk out of plastic bottles – some of which made it onto cereal – and made cups of tea. As bacon sizzled and sliced sausage looked unhealthily attractive in their little pools of future heart problems, we all watched Harry eat his cornflake and brown sauce roll. There are a number of adjectives one might deploy to describe the sight of a youth eating such a thing; the one I'd choose is phlegmatic. We asked both as a group and individually why he'd chosen as he had for breakfast, but he seemed content with his decision. As if to assuage our concerns or possibly deflect them, he up-ended the squeezy sauce bottle and directed a jet of its contents into his face. We assume he was aiming for his mouth and missed or there was a fault with the nozzle – we're still not sure. In any case, after that, breakfast was consumed with the usual levels of aplomb and we set about packing up for the day's journey.

With kit stowed and keys for the microcabins handed back to reception, we began the road trip section of our expedition. We had no accommodation booked for the rest of the trip, although we had checked online so had some options in rough proximity to our destination for the day, which was Dunnet Head on the north coast. Between Invermoriston and Thurso, which was where we eventually did find ourselves that evening, there was plenty to do and see. Looking back, in our enthusiasm to cover so much ground, the overall experience was probably poorer for it. I mean, we were in a minibus so weren't flying exactly, but it was too easy to pass a place without exploring it. Since we also hadn't yet confirmed a firm destination for the coming night, we wanted to have some daylight in hand in case we ended up having to hunt around for a suitable place to stay. There is a campsite at John O'Groats but we knew it would be closed, so the other possible option we knew about was Brough Bay, but having camped there before on a motor cycle trip, I didn't think there would be enough space for us all, plus, our minibus would struggle to get down the single track road. Add in to that, like the John O'Groats site, most other campsites were either closed or not suitable for Scouts to use. I'm not making it up when I say we've been on trips where we've turned up at campsites and the owners have seen us approach and closed their blinds, literally – we could hear locks snicking into place. All of this was ahead of us though, so first order of the day was to get on the road and have a good look at Loch Ness as we trundled along its banks toward Inverness where we'd be stopping to resupply for the days ahead.

There is more water in Loch Ness than there is in all of the lakes in England and Wales combined. It's also the second deepest loch in the British Isles with a depth of 733 feet or 230 metres. Loch Morar near Oban on the west coast of Scotland is the deepest, plunging to depths of 1017 feet or 310 metres.

It goes without saying, lochs with depths as generous as these also have monsters in attendance: Loch Ness has Nessie, whereas Loch Morar's cryptozoological horror is known as Morag. It's fair to say, the local area around Loch Ness has cashed in generously on the possible existence of a monster. Several documentaries and films have been made about it, arguably peaking with PolyGram Filmed Entertainment's motion picture aptly named *Loch Ness*, starring Hollywood legend Ted Danson. I think we can all agree that if they've made a film about a thing and a film industry heavyweight such as Danson deemed it worthy of his involvement, you've pretty much cemented that thing's place in history. I mean, come on now – Ted Danson...

As for the Great Glen Way route itself, after Fort Augustus, it mostly wends its way along the tops of the hills to the north of Loch Ness on forestry paths then on B class roads. We would see it again later that day as we passed through Invermoriston, then again in Drumnadrochit and finally as it crossed the Tomnahurich Swing Bridge on the outskirts of Inverness.

Invermoriston is a picturesque village clustered round the River Moriston before it empties into Loch Ness – it's also a place we'd see again later in the week as we looped back from points further north. I'm sure you might already know, when a place name has *inver* or *aber* as a beginning, it usually means it's situated at a confluence of water courses or where a river meets a larger water body. *Inver* has its roots in the Gaelic *inbhir* while *aber* has its basis in Common Brittonic. ('What else?' I hear you exclaim.) More commonly and simplistically, either word could be said to mean a river mouth. I only offer this information because if you know someone who is a bit gobby or has a big mouth, you could postfix their name with *aber* or *inver* behind their backs.

The focal point of Invermoriston is the Glenmoriston Hotel, an attractive whitewashed building which overlooks the road from Kyle of Lochalsh and Skye as it joins the main Inverness-to-Fort William road. There is also a post office and general store and an exceedingly photogenic Thomas Telford Bridge built in 1813 over the positively itching-to-be-photographed River Moriston Falls. You can get a cup of coffee and a slice of cake in the village, and for those with an interest in clogs, there is a gift shop that sells finely crafted yet keenly priced examples of the footwear and a lot else besides, much of which is crafted on site. As we glided majestically by in our minibus, which had yet more warning lights illuminated on the dashboard, howls of dissent could be heard from the back seats as we failed to stop.

Next on the road is the youth hostel at Alltsigh, which is a viable place to stay – as much as any youth hostel could be said to be viable. If you're walking this stretch of the Great Glen Way, the route drops down to within easy reach of the main road and the hostel with its bus stop. I have no idea why, but the hostel is only open during peak months. You would think, given its position, it would be open all year round, but alas no, it remains resolutely closed between August and May. Also, in keeping with Youth Hostel Association eccentricity around rules, its doors are locked between 10am and 5pm, meaning inmates – sorry, I mean patrons – have to bugger off out for the day. Despite that, TripAdvisor ratings (if you ignore those who confuse hostel accommodation with B&B or hotel accommodation) are rather good. Alas, we've never been in so couldn't possibly comment.

Onwards to the neighbouring villages of Lewiston and Drumnadrochit, which constitute the most substantial conurbation on the banks of Loch Ness. The main road hugs the hillside close to the loch while the route of the Great Glen Way follows a parallel course high above in pleasantly mixed woodland and eventually onto a minor road at a place called Grotaig. The main road curves round the headland near to Castle Urquhart whereas the walking route above cuts the corner and drops down into Lewiston. Walkers can choose to follow a moderate dog-leg via Clunebeg Lodge or stay on the minor road which zigzags steeply down, regaining the route proper in due course. Contrary to what some websites and guides imply about the Great Glen Way, you can't see Castle Urquhart from the route – you can't even see it from the road. If you want to visit the castle, you need to pay the entrance fee and for a family of four – how best to explain it? You know if you're raking around in a cupboard and you notice out the corner of your eye what turns out to be a giant hairy house spider in one corner? That dawning realisation is much the same as that which you feel when you discover what the entrance fee is, and because you're right there at the reception desk surrounded by people, if you don't cough up, everyone will think you're a miserly git. It's very much a double whammy.

Hotels, B&Bs, cafés and shops abound in Lewiston and Drumnadrochit. There is a decent-sized Cooperative Store if you need to stock up on Haribo (which we did) and a collection of cafés and gift shops in a pleasant square in Drumnadrochit itself. As you pass the Cooperative Store on the left coming into 'Drum', you'll also notice a collection of sports fields, most of which are attached to Glen Urquhart High and Primary school. You may notice one has had installed some oddly shaped, overly square-looking goal posts – these belong to the Glen Urquhart Shinty Club who play their home games there. You may think hockey, stereotypically described as a game for girls (while the boys play rugby) is pretty rough – shinty takes it to another level. In hockey, all sticks are right-handed, so players can only hit the ball with one side, proffering a certain predictability (if only imagined) to the trajectory a hockey stick might take as it cleaves through the air. In shinty they use both sides, meaning sticks are often swung back and forth, which in addition to being swung wildly above head height should the occasion require it, adds a whole new tang hockey players rarely enjoy. Jolly hockey sticks to one side, you have to be a hardy sort to play hockey – those who play shinty on the other hand are quite mad.

If you wish to find out more about the Loch Ness Monster, Drumnadrochit is the place to do it. Next door to the Drumnadrochit Hotel (an uninspiring 1980s-style building) you'll find The Loch Ness Centre and Exhibition. You won't be surprised to know we didn't go in, so we can't say if it's good or bad – it does get good write-ups though. A series of displays with artefacts and exhibits can be viewed as you walk round the old building, which used to be a hotel.

It is interesting to note, the first people to claim they'd seen a monster – as reported by water bailiff and Courier reporter Alex Campbell – was a Mrs Aldie Mackay, who was the manageress of the Drumnadrochit Hotel at the time of the sighting in May of 1933, and her husband. Some time later that year, in July as it happens, a chap called George Spicer and his dear lady were driving along the banks of Loch Ness when 'a most extraordinary form of animal' passed in front of their motor car and into the waters of the loch. Then again, a month later, a motorcyclist attributed his 1am crash to avoiding a similar beast crossing the road to access the waters of Loch Ness. It is not known if any of these people were on their way home from the Drumnadrochit Hotel bar.

Nessie's status as the UK's Number One Cryptid was assured in 1934 when a photo, said to have been taken by a Robert Kenneth Wilson, seemed to show a broken bit of wood sticking up out of the water. You've probably seen it – it's the most famous image of Nessie (Ted Danson blockbusters to one side) in existence. Even so, only with a liberal application of imagination could it be said to be the humped body, long neck and small head of a monster. The picture, dubbed 'The Surgeon's Photograph' (because Wilson was a prominent London gynaecologist), was published in the Daily Mail in 1934 – which to my mind makes it a definite fake. And so it turned out to be when the truth came to light in the 1990s. It's an entertaining yarn and worth recounting. After various sightings in the run up to 1934, the Daily Mail newspaper decided to cash in on the craze. It would pay big game hunter Marmaduke Wetherell to find evidence of the monster. Duke Wetherill searched diligently, seemingly to no avail, but eventually found giant footprints that could only belong to one thing. Well, two things, actually: Nessie or a hippopotamus, or more accurately according to researchers at the Natural History Museum, a deceased hippopotamus who's left hind foot had been turned into an umbrella stand. It's not clear if Wetherell created the footprints or a local joker did, either way Wetherell was publicly ridiculed then sacked by the paper (imagine being sacked by the Daily Mail – the ignominy).

Equal parts mortified and cross, Wetherell got in touch with Christian Spurling, who was a sculpture specialist, as well as his son-in-law, his own son Ian Wetherell, and a friend named Maurice Chambers. He asked Spurling to create a model which could be attached to a model submarine bought from Woolworths by Ian Wetherell. Once built, the group travelled to Loch Ness with their contraption so the photos could be taken.

Surgeon Robert Wilson (and again, accounts differ) was either a keen practical joker (as are most gynaecologists of note, as we all know) or a willing front man who would lend a certain credence to events. In any case, he didn't take the photos. Wetherell did – from the Altsaigh Tea House, which has to be near to if not now be the Alltsigh Hostel mentioned earlier. He then passed one photo to Wilson who in turned passed it on to the Daily Mail who made it famous to this day.

All of this came out in 1994, when Christian Spurling, on his deathbed, gave a stilted account of the goings on. The original uncropped photo can be found on www.hoaxes.org (search for 'the surgeon's photo'). When you see it in context (with the ripples on the water and the far bank of the loch), it's easy to work out that whatever it was, it was no monster.

While the gang of hoaxers were taking their photos, a water bailiff was heard approaching. Duke Wetherall sank the model with his foot, and it was never recovered – it's still down there somewhere, lurking…

Wilson didn't want his name associated with the photo which is why it became known as 'The surgeons photo' and was later heard to mutter to himself, 'The Daily-bloody-Mail? I'm not having my name printed in that rag! Why didn't I try for a broadsheet, you blithering idiot?' (I'm joking – I made that up.) Be that as it may, many other sightings have been reported. In November of 1933, some months before the waggish Dr Wilson embarked upon his jape, a fellow called Hugh Gray snapped several photos of something causing a stir in the water. As is the way of these things, only one came out and even then not in a way that made the beast's existence unequivocal – there are those who say it was a picture of his labrador retriever swimming in the loch with a stick in its mouth. But wait, don't go yet, because in 1938 a South African tourist called GE Taylor claimed to have filmed the monster – three minutes on 16mm film no less. The film came into the possession of zoologist and popular scientist Maurice Burton, who featured one frame from the film in his book, but wouldn't let any other investigators see the video. Since Burton was a sceptic who did not think the monster was real, it seems obvious to me that the video does indeed contain hard evidence and Burton was just miffed to be wrong about it.

Since then, several sighting have been reported: in 1938, 1943 and 1954. In 1960, Nessie hunter Tim Dinsdale on his last day of searching (I know) filmed a hump that 'left a powerful wake'. Dinsdale described the object as being red with a blotch on its side, and apparently the Joint Air Reconnaissance Intelligence Centre – part of the UK Defence Intelligence Agency at the time – thought it was 'animate'. Unfortunately, others said if you increased the resolution you could see it was a boat with a man standing in it. Gordon Holmes, a fifty-five-year-old lab technician shot footage of a 'jet black thing' moving fairly fast in the water in 2007, which made it onto the news. Adrian Shine, a marine biologist at the Loch Ness Centre and Exhibition, said it was the best footage he'd ever seen. Although later in a TV interview, he said it could have been an otter, seal or sea bird. Later still it emerged that Gordon Holmes had a history of reporting sightings of cryptozoological animals and had a self-published book and DVD claiming evidence for the existence of fairies…

Various other photos and videos of the monster have been reported, all of which have been promoted as real by those who snapped them and dismissed as logs, seals or gusts of wind by those who think it's all bullshit. I for one think the monster is real. The waters of Loch Ness are very dark and you only need to be as little as six feet down before you are taken by the stygian blackness. It goes without saying, any animal that has become accustomed to such darkness couldn't come to the surface, at least not without sunglasses, and where would a beast like Nessie get a pair of those?

There are two other important things for the keen tourist to know about Drumnadrochit: it is the second most Scottish sounding place name after Auchtermuchty, and there is a model (possibly life-sized) of Nessie in a pond next to the exhibition centre beside which you can have your photo taken. Equally, you could stop somewhere along the road, chuck a log in the water and take a picture with that in the background – it's what everyone else seems to be doing.

Onwards past Drumnadrochit, we whizzed past the Loch Ness Clansman Hotel, with its small harbour opposite, and then past the bottom of the road for Abriachan. Abriachan is described as a village, but it's really a collection of crofts and remote homes spread out on the hillside as it rises above the banks of the loch. In terms of the Great Glen Way, the turn off for Abriachan is also the road to take if you wanted to access the last stretches of the route by car.

Soon after leaving Drumnadrochit, the route of the Great Glen Way wends its way steeply up into the woods above the road and pops out above a small body of water called Loch Laide, then once over a minor road, it enters woodland again and passes very close to the Abriachan Eco-Campsite.

We passed through a couple of years previously when the campsite was very much a work in progress, with a lot of building going on.

Walkers could get a hot chocolate and bit of shortbread or if they required something more substantial, maybe a cheese toastie. Animals seemed to wander freely, with pigs, chickens and large dogs that looked like wolves roaming around – although they were half-heartedly corralled behind a rickety metal fence. The owners, when we met them, were friendly and very busy building. We liked it immensely because it was all a bit disorganised. Sandra the owner was wearing a bin liner as an overcoat and a broad smile – she insisted we have our photo taken for their Facebook page, which we did happily. The campsite is 19 miles shy of Inverness so is a good stop off point, although if you're walking with a novice group, it does leave a longer final day, but it is easy walking and mostly down hill.

If you're using the British Waterways campsites, there is a final site between Loch Ness and Inverness; unfortunately, it is a number of miles off the route, located at the canal locks in a place called Dochgarroch. The toilet and drying facilities are on the north side of the locks, with the campsite itself being a little less obvious on the south side. You need transport to get to Dochgarroch, and since Inverness is almost as close, and offers a wider array of options (like pubs, restaurants and shops), it renders Dochgarroch somewhat moot. After Dochgarroch Lock, there are a further six locks in Inverness that lower the canal to sea level and into the Beauly Firth. The route of the Great Glen Way, terminating as it does in the centre of Inverness, doesn't touch any of these final locks, although your keys, if you have them, will open toilets and showers at Seaport Marina just before the canal meets the salty waters of the Firth.

The Great Glen Way does rejoin the canal for a few hundred feet just outside town then veers away from the canal for the last time at the Tomnahurich Swing Bridge. From there, it's only a mile or two to the finish point in the grounds of Inverness Castle in the centre of town.

(Since completing this trip, we've walked the Great Glen Way in its entirety. Along the way we visited Nessieland (not to be confused with the Loch Ness Centre and Exhibition) and the tourist shops attached and can confirm there is an awful lot of tat for sale. We also stayed the night at the Abriachan Eco-campsite – it was a great night with campfire songs and guitar music. Unfortunately, the site has no facilities. The water supply is a twenty minute walk away, and the toilets, well, to say they were basic would be to talk them up. I thought it was funny but others not so much so. The tent pitches were few and far between – people were turning up with nowhere to pitch their tents even though they had booked. A French dad and his son walking the Great Glen Way abandoned their tent in the middle of the night and left, possibly in disgust. The only evidence of their passing through was their sodden part-fallen tent sitting in the shallow pond their pitch had become sometime during the night – I felt bad for them. As campsites go, in terms of the basics, well, it didn't even have any of those. What I found particularly challenging about it was they charged full whack. I'm all for making the most of an interesting situation, but it seemed they expected us to hack a tent pitch out of the primal forest itself. I think anyone would agree, if you're running a campsite, you sort of need to have – oh, I don't know – a campsite on which to pitch tents? One surprise, however, was the British Waterway campsite at Dochgarroch. You should go there because not only was it better than the Abriachan Eco-campsite but also it's the best of all the British Waterway campsites, having as it does all the usual facilities plus great access, picnic tables and good ground on which to pitch tents.)

It was over the Tomnahurich Swing Bridge we trundled in our minibus to Inverness. We weren't stopping in the town centre; instead, we were heading for the large superstore squatting in the unimaginatively and slightly depressingly named Inverness Retail and Leisure Park. You might be surprised to know that this particular store – we'll call it a Tesco because that is what it was – at one time was the largest in Scotland. I know what you're thinking: 'Don't be silly, Inverness is tiny compared to the urban conurbations in Scotland's central belt. Why did it have the biggest Tesco ever?' For the first ten years of the 21st century, Inverness experienced serious growth with a population increase of close to 18% between 2003 and 2013*, at the time it was one of Europe's fastest growing cities. Inverness (or Inversneckie as it is affectionately known by locals) was afforded city status in 2000, gamely fighting off competition from Ayr, Paisley and Stirling. It also experienced enviable economic growth; in the ten years to 2008 there was an 86% increase in average economic productivity in the wider Highland region†, then that thing happened with the banks and it ground to a halt. Even so, economists who understand these things would agree it was somewhat beneficial. In 2007, a bigger Tesco was built in Port Glasgow (in the central belt), robbing Inverness of that accolade, although it's not known if anyone noticed.

* National Records of Scotland mid-year estimates 2003 and 2013

† Bank Of Scotland research via the BBC

Hence, the still-cavernous Tesco anchored in one corner of the vast retail park. Leaders Number Two and Three immediately saw the problem; not only would the torture of choice rear its head again but our young charges would be paralysed by the scale of the shop. I mean it's nice to have a bit of choice, but if you have to trawl along miles of shelving continually assaulted from the left and right by colourful packaging that screams, 'BUY ME, BUY ME, BUY ME', it's not conducive to a quick shopping trip. I had images of adolescents struck dumb by the sheer range on offer, unable to move so just turning gently on the spot staring glassy-eyed at the pretty packaging that had coalesced into a roiling kaleidoscopic mass.

With strict instructions to focus on buying lunch and dinner for today and breakfast for tomorrow then be back at the van by midday, we watched them wander off across the vast car park already looking somewhat lost.

Readers should probably understand that the words in the previous two paragraphs are tempered by my own views of large out-of-town superstores. It's very possible – probable even – that the young folk weren't in the least bit intimidated and I've projected my own anxieties about these mega-store shops onto them.

While our crew shopped, us leaders had planned to visit the in-store café for some breakfast – for in the morning's rush we'd missed out. What we found was the usual café had been replaced by some sort of faux posh coffee shop/restaurant. When you go to a supermarket during the day, who do you normally see in the café? Old folk, pensioners out for a wee bit of shopping and a cup of tea with a pal, that's who, or as in our case, road weary travellers looking for a bacon roll and a cup of coffee. Who goes to a supermarket to do a weekly shop then sit down to a Happy Vegan Salad or a Chipotle Nacho Chicken Burger or a Falafel, Feta and Roasted Red Pepper Quesadilla. I mean, what is a quesadilla, and who's ever met a happy vegan? It's a Tesco superstore not London's Soho, Glasgow's Merchant City or Livingston's…well, never mind. The place – called Giraffe - even had a bar. Not that I am averse to such things, but in a superstore? It made no sense to us, so much so that we filled out a comments form and put it in the suggestions box. We mentioned the confused OAPs looking for the familiar café; we said weary travellers didn't want trendy metrosexual rabbit food, they wanted a sliced sausage roll; we pointed out having miserable looking vegans gnawing on twigs in the window as potential customers walked by probably wouldn't be good for business – well, maybe not that last one, but still, we were bemused and wanted them to know it.

Instead we did some food shopping of our own. So far we'd had chicken, beef and mince with pasta, rice and more pasta. That evening we decided on beef in a black bean sauce with rice, which we all agreed was suitably adventurous without being overly challenging. We were planning to wild camp that night, so we also bought bottled water in addition to the water container we had with us, which we'd filled back at the microcabins. We'd talked about it and decided on Dunnet Head because from memory there was plenty of space and some shelter to be had – it was also miles away from anywhere so we assumed we'd be left alone. That said, wild camping in October is not for the faint hearted, so I'd already been looking online for alternative campsites, most of which were closed for the season; or hostels, which on the north coast were few and far between. Still, like the good Scouts we were, we were prepared to rough it if necessary.

As we wandered around the vast space of the Inverness Retail and Leisure Park Tesco, every now and again we'd see in the distance our group. They seemed to be sticking together for safety – which I felt was wise. We finished our shopping and returned to the minibus, scowling at the Giraffe restaurant on the way out. With no sign of our young folk appearing anytime soon, I decided to repack the group equipment in a more organised fashion. The system we had with the two storage boxes we'd bought in Fort William was working well, but adolescents being what they were meant items were being chucked in randomly. Personal kit was being stored on the back row of seats – taking care to make sure it didn't block the back door – while food and group equipment was stored on the front bench seat – again, while trying not to block the side door. As we drove, every now and again there would be a small avalanche of gear as things settled, and the side door would become blocked. It doesn't help that young people like to rake, and while doing so leave in their wake a state of disarray, which completely destroys any pre-existing system of order meant to prevent collapse.

There are those who claim it's impossible to understand what its like having kids if you've never had kids of your own, but that isn't strictly true because it's possible to borrow other people's children for a spell. It might be hard to accept, but sometimes the young folk think I'm grumpy. I accept this charge, mostly because it's true, in fact, I'd question the 'sometimes' bit and change it to 'very often' or 'all the time'. Every now and again, Peak-Grump – a new phrase I'm coining – is reached when I've spent a fair bit of time achieving a certain objective (usually something of fleeting importance) and the young people arrive, ignore it completely, then ruin it. It's probably not even that important, it's just me being awkward and possibly a little pedantic – and at that moment outside Tesco – still being a little exercised by the whole Giraffe thing.

After a time, Explorer Scouts trickled back in groups of two or three – it is a rule of thumb that young people while shopping will remain together until they are at the checkouts, at which point they'll realise they've forgotten something vital. Someone – usually the one most likely to get lost, way-laid or distracted – will be sent to retrieve the missing item and won't be seen for up to an hour. Over the course of thirty minutes as young people appeared, a haphazard pyramid of poorly bagged shopping grew a-top my innovative and daring minibus storage paradigm. When the last fiend returned, nonchalantly flinging over their shoulder a final bag onto my now ruined equipment storage system, they regarded my deep frown with innocent curiosity.

Whether it's down to their easy going nature or because they are all so unwaveringly nice, it is impossible to remain grumpy for long with these young folk. I repacked the shopping with equanimity and wondered why they'd bought quite so many Matteson's Smoked Pork Sausages.

While there are those who may say Inverness is in the north of Scotland, it is more accurate to say it's toward the north of Scotland. There are another 120 miles or so from Inverness to the north coast of the Scottish mainland at John O'Groats, and another 215 miles from there to Skaw on the Isle of Unst in the Shetland Islands – the most northerly settlement in Scotland. Scotland may look satisfyingly bulky but it is really quite skinny: from its border with England at Gretna Green, it is 90 miles to Edinburgh and another

156 miles from Edinburgh to Inverness. Meanwhile, at its narrowest – between the Firths of Forth and Clyde – Scotland has a waistline of a mere 25 miles. Scotland's widest point of 156 miles as the crow flies (or 186 miles by road) lies between Applecross in the west to Buchan Ness in the east – a line that passes through Inverness.

Travelling north, we left Inverness on the A9 and arrived on the Black Isle via the Kessock Bridge, a bridge that is often described as iconic, forming as it does an integral part of the Inverness skyline (especially in the evening when it is illuminated). Spanning the Beauly Firth, the road deck sits 29 metres above the water, with the four towers – standing on piles driven 60 metres into the seabed, topping out another 40 metres above that. The Great Glen Fault, of which the Beauly Firth is a continuation, was formed by a strike-slip or transcurrent fault that exists deep underground. The land to the north of the fault is moving – albeit very slowly – toward Scandinavia, while the land to the south is heading the other way completely. With that slight movement in mind, the Kessock Bridge has two four-hundred-tonne hydraulic buffers built into its northern abutment to deal with the tiny amount of movement that occurs each year.

While interesting, I'd be lying if I said any of that was at the forefront of my mind let alone those of the Explorers as we passed over the bridge and onwards toward that evening's destination – wherever that may be.

I was going to say we were now skimming across the surface of the Black Isle, but you don't skim anywhere in a loaded minibus, you lurch and rattle. However, it wouldn't be the only misrepresentation because the Black Isle isn't an island, it's a peninsula, and nor is it black. To the north and south you have the Cromarty and Beauly firths respectively, to the east there is North Sea and to the west a latticework of rivers and streams. The land is attractively verdant with little sign of industry that might suggest a darker hue in the past – from coal extraction say. That said, on the Cromarty Firth there's a fair bit of oil industry activity, but it was known as the Black Isle long before the advent of petrochemicals. According to roughguides.com, the name might refer to the areas milder climate where frosts are rare so fields are always black, or alternatively that it's a derivation of St Duthus (as in 'dubh' which is the Gaelic word for black) about whom you will see several mentions if you happen to be rattling around the area.

With plenty to see and do in the area, one might visit the Black Isle Brewery near Munlochy (not ideal with a youth group, right enough) or head for Avoch or Chanonry point to look at some dolphins. To the north east, the village of Cromarty sits on the tip of the Black Isle peninsula where in the summer months there is a ferry service to Balnapaling on the northern shore of the Cromarty Firth. The drive along the minor road to Cromarty gives good views of oil industry activity in the firth: several oil rigs lay waiting to be decommissioned and an impressively large pipe laying vessel, the

Apache II, has its home on the northern shore. This particular vessel's speciality is (and I quote) '…laying reeled rigid pipe up to 16" diameter, in water depths to 1,500 m, and a range of pipe-in-pipe and Electrically Trace Heated PiP products…'. If you're looking to lay some pipe up to 16 inches in diameter or some PiP products on the ocean's floor, you now know where to go.

You're welcome.

Leaving the Black Isle to the north, you pass over the austere and business-like Cromarty Bridge. The road passes Culbokie on the right and the sign for Conon Bridge on the left and swoops down to cross the western limits of the Cromarty Firth – the bridge itself is long and low and curves gracefully to the northern shore. Passing the elongated settlement of Evanton on one side, you can see on the other more evidence of oil industry activity – the area is highly dependant on the oil sector for jobs. Then the villages of Alness, Invergordon, Tomich and Kildary all flew past our windows.

The next substantial settlement on the road north is a place called Tain. The A9 skirts round the edges but if you want to stop for an iPhone charger, Tain has within its environs the last sizeable supermarkets. If it's a pie you're after, you could try your luck at one of the many corner shops or Cooperatives on the road or you could nip in to William Grant's Bakery on the High Street in Tain. I spent a fortnight in Tain working and can confirm their pies thoroughly deserved the Silver award they earned at the 2013 Scotch Pie

Awards – I know, Scotch Pie Awards… isn't it a wonderful time to be alive?

As I was saying to the clearly interested young people in the minibus, the area around Tain is a bit of a hidden gem. There are no roller coasters or strip clubs but if it's the bucolic life you like, you could do worse than a weekend in an area which abounds with walks and interesting things to look at. Mind you, I would avoid the area to the east of the town beyond the golf course, sometimes known as RAF Tain or RNAS Tain, as it's now a bombing range controlled by the Defence Training Estate. No live bombs are dropped these days (that all happens at Cape Wrath) but the RAF still drop 3kg and 14kg 'practice' bombs and the occasional 'inert' 1000lb concrete bomb – although just how inert a thing weighing a tonne and dropped from any sort of height from the bottom of an aircraft travelling at 500mph is debatable.

Portmahomack – apart from being winsomely named – is a quaint fishing village to the east of Tain on the road to Tarbet Ness Lighthouse, the third tallest in Scotland (after North Ronaldsay and Skerryvore, if you're interested). It's a Stevenson built affair standing 153ft tall with two red bands round its girth. The walk out is also quite nice with views to the Black Isle in the south and to Dornoch, Embo, Skelbo and Golspie in the north – including a faint impression of the still controversial statue commemorating the Duke of Sutherland, who was by many accounts, a bit of a bastard – but we'll get to that.

Leaving Tain (and passing the famous Glen Morangie distillery) we passed over another long low bridge spanning the Dornoch Firth. Before this bridge was built travellers had to travel up the northern shore of the firth to cross at Bonar Bridge. The bridge at Bonar spans the Kyle of the rivers Oykel, Cassley, Shin and Carron. (In case you're interested and/or weren't sure, a *kyle* is the Scottish name for a narrow or strait, usually filled with water, sometimes navigable.) The water course separates Ross and Cromarty to the south with Sutherland to the north and empties into the Dornoch Firth. The current bridge spanning the Kyle of Sutherland was opened in 1973, replacing among others a bridge designed by Thomas Telford that was swept away in a flood in 1892. Apparently the Brahan Seer (also prosaically known as Kenneth Mackenzie) foresaw this. Ken (as I like to call him) was a 'predictor of the future' who lived in the 1700s on the Black Isle where we'd just been. He was something of a wit but also used an Adder Stone (a stone with a naturally formed hole in it) to predict the future. Unfortunately, through the hole Ken claimed to see his employer – another Kenneth Mackenzie, 3rd Earl of Seaforth – doing a fair bit of philandering while on business in France. The Lady Seaforth decided to shoot the messenger and had poor Ken jammed into a spiked and tarred barrel and set on fire, which I think we can all agree is a good deal harsher than appearing on The Jeremy Kyle Show. Topically, before being burned alive, Seer Ken also foresaw boats sailing round the back of 'Tomnahurich Hill', and if you've been paying any attention at all, you'll recall we crossed the Tomnahurich Swing Bridge on the western outskirts of

Inverness, where the Caledonian Canal, after having split from the River Ness, goes round the back of Tomnahurich Hill.

It's an interesting and moderately spectacular prediction, but there are also those who believe much of the Brahan Seer Story was made up by a fellow called Alexander Mackenzie. He was a magazine editor, author and historian born on a croft near Gairloch in 1838 who then moved to Inverness in 1869 – long after the Caledonian Canal opened for business – including the bit that goes round the back of Tomnahurich Hill.

Travelling ever northwards across the Dornoch Firth into Sutherland took us past Clashmore, Evalix and Poles among other small hamlets, neatly bypassing the coastal villages of Dornoch (quite nice), Embo (twinned with Kaunakakai on the island of Molokai in Hawaii), Fourpenny and Skelbo (both quite picturesque). I've visited Embo and have no idea why it is twinned with a village in Hawaii – unless they block off lovely beaches with unlovely caravan parks too. I couldn't (for example) see any palm trees and when I visited no smiling residents were on hand to place leis around visitor's necks, so it must be the ugly caravan parks.

The main A9 road meets the minor road from Dornoch and Embo at Loch Fleet and The Mound – of which more in a minute. If you have the time, there are two good reasons to detour onto the coast road for Dornoch and Embo: you can have your photo taken at the very Hawaiian-looking sign there and lie to friends and family about your summer holiday, and the drive up Loch Fleet's southern shore back to the main road is very nice indeed.

Loch Fleet is home to many wading birds and although it looks like a barren mud flat when the tide is out, apparently it teems with life. Worms, larvae and other tiny sea creatures left by the receding tide fester and glisten in the mud, and when the tide is in, all manner of aquatic life (and the worms) support a veritable plethora of bird life – or so the information board said.

The Mound – over which the A9 passes – is a 1000ft long earthen rampart designed by Thomas Telford and finished in June of 1816, as part of the process to cut journey times for travellers in conjunction with the bridges at Bonar and Helmsdale. They couldn't just build a causeway because the extent of the incoming tide meant the high mark was a mile beyond plus the River Fleet needed somewhere to go. Originally four sluice gates were built into The Mound but that was later increased to six. Each arch contains a sluice gate that is self-regulated; when the tide is high it stops seawater advancing and when the tide begins to ebb, river water is allowed to flow out. The A9 no longer passes over the old bridge holding up the original arches as a new bridge has since been built. Like us, you can stop and park down by the old bridge and have a good poke around. There are picnic benches around which you can have lunch and for the more advanced in years, several information boards to peruse.

It's a measure of just how nice a vista is if a young person notices. Rhianna, who admittedly is a keen photographer so has an eye for a view, noticed and took some photos. Everyone else had lunch, threw stones off the old bridge in the sluice pool and took the opportunity to water the bushes.

With lunch finished, the van packed and back on the road north, there was something of a shadow over our shoulders. Perched a-top Ben Bhraggie above the village of Golspie is the statue of George Leveson-Gower, Marquess of Stafford and First Duke of Sutherland, also known as the notorious bastard responsible for a lot of the highland clearances in the area. A story of privilege and oppression – typical of the day – he was a British Member of Parliament for Newcastle-under-Lyme and later for Staffordshire, at one point ambassador to France (having no diplomatic experience) then Joint Postmaster General. He was also a member of the House of Lords, mostly a Tory but laterally a Whig; the rest of his CV is just as you'd expect: honours from the British Establishment thrown like confetti, twice a lord lieutenant, a privy counsellor, a Night of the Garter and a Duke.

He married the Countess Elizabeth Sutherland in 1785, and part of that arrangement was that he'd gain control (but not ownership) of the Sutherland estates. After buying more land and extending the scope of the estate, they came to own between them two thirds of Sutherland, and George - in his own right - was said to be the richest man alive in the 19th century.

Between 1811 and 1820, clearances took place. Subsistence farmers were moved from their inland farms to the coast where it was assumed they'd take up fishing. These were poor farmers already struggling, but although it was no highland idyll, they survived. However, the land they farmed in the glens could be more profitably used to farm sheep. Hence, the farmers and their families were moved onto much smaller, less fertile plots close to the sea. While some were offered jobs on these new super-sheep farms at jaw-droppingly low rates of pay, others were expected to farm what they could on rocky coastal plots that not even sheep could graze, and fish for the rest. These clearances were not unique to the highlands of Scotland. As far south as the Isle of Arran, tenant farmers were forced off the land and to the coast to make way for sheep farming – this was said to be an 'improvement' by the rich landowning classes. In truth, they just didn't understand how people lived in the Scottish glens.

This was enforced with ruthless disregard for life. One of Sutherland's factors was acquitted of murder – a croft was set alight while it still contained one Margaret MacKay who'd refused to leave. The factor later took over a huge sheep farm created by the clearances he'd helped carry out – you can well imagine the resentment in the area.

In 1837, a statue of the Duke of Sutherland was erected in his memory (he died in 1833) on Ben Bhraggie, but despite locals wanting it removed to this day, it still stands above Golspie.

As shadows go, it's a long one. The classic view of the Scottish glen is not a natural one – land management over centuries has produced many of the iconic views you might see on postcards today. You can't shoot grouse and pheasant, or stalk deer in a forest, so the trees had to go. The various types of big birds of prey that used to be native to Scotland couldn't co-exist with sheep farming; newly born lambs are easily carried away by golden eagles. Similarly wild lynx have always been seen as a threat to farm animals so have been systematically eradicated. In 2013, it was thought only thirty-five remained in the wild.

Pine martins, red squirrels, black grouse and many more besides have been poisoned or blasted to, or very near to, extinction in Scotland over the past 300 years, usually by braying estate-owning posh boys and their cronies. So it's gladdening to know they're thinking about reintroducing wolves and bears into the wilds of Scotland. Granted, ramblers, hill walkers and Duke of Edinburgh Awardees will need to keep their eyes open but I think we can all agree, the notion of a group of overly entitled gun-toting gas-bags being stalked by a pack of hungry wolves or being chased by a pissed-off bear is a price worth paying.

North of Golspie past the small village of Brora, you can see the clearance memorial on the southern outskirts of Helmsdale, and it's worth visiting. Even now, it is a defining aspect of Scottish history in the area; there are those who think of it as ethnic cleansing and not without reason. Whatever we might think, it deserves to be remembered for what it was: a deeply unsavoury episode visited upon Scotland by a ruling class whose only concern was profit.

The village of Helmsdale is still 50 miles short of John O' Groats, so we still had a distance to cover. We trundled through the small linear settlements of Navidale, Ousdale, Berriedale, Newport, Borgue and Ramsdale and all the while over to our right was an endless sea vista only occasionally punctuated by an oil drilling platform. Eventually even the main route north, the A9, loses interest and veers north toward Thurso while we continued eastwards on the A99 at Latheron. Every few hundred yards neat little bungalows attended by out buildings, sheep and stunning sea vistas dotted the rolling countryside. We passed through curiously named places such as Lybster, Ulbster and Thrumster until our wheezing minibus with its steamed up windows eventually hove to in the urban sprawl of Wick. It's fair to say Wick is in the middle of nowhere, but is surrounded by history. The Old Castle of Wick or the remains of it at least, date back to the 12th century when the area was part of Harald Maddadson's Norwegian Earldom of Orkney, although all that's left is a single tower standing on cliffs to the south of Wick itself. Travellers who also frequent the pub might be familiar with the name Old Pulteney. This is a form of déjà vu unique to Scotland. You'll be travelling through an area and will see signposted a town or village whose name you will swear you've seen somewhere before even though you've never previously set foot in the area. It's further complicated by the notion you probably saw it on a shelf in a bar while in a state of some disrepair – and so it is with Old Pulteney, which is a well-regarded single malt produced in and named after a suburb of Wick. If you want to be one of 'those' people in the pub, The Old Pulteney is so named because the distillery sits in Pulteneytown named after Sir William Pulteney, 5th Baronet, who was a landowner, politician and stinking rich patron of Robert Adam (who designed and built many stately piles) and Thomas Telford (who built most of everything else). Sir William, 5th Baronet – or Bill as I like to call him – in his capacity as the governor of the British Fisheries Society, enlisted Thomas Telford to design a new village and harbour that would at the time be the largest herring fishing settlement in Britain. It was expected to be populated by people who'd been thrown off their tenant farms during the clearances – although to be fair to Bill, he died in 1805, which was a good bit before landowners became ornery during the second and arguably more brutal phase of the Highland Clearances.

Wick is a good supply point and hub, with decent shops and a train station linking the town to Thurso on the north coast. Also – and I think you'll find this is the clincher in terms of deciding to visit – in 2006 the world's media reported that the Guinness Book of World Records had declared Wick's Ebenezer Place the shortest street in the world. I know, Wick truly is a magical place. At 6ft 9in (a meagre 2.06 metres) the street only has one door and were it not for its recognised postal address (in existence since 1883 when it was constructed) it would otherwise be thought of as a junction. In fact, it's so small, when we passed through we didn't even know it was there, although I'm sure if the young people had, they would have insisted we stop so they could take a selfie, which I have no doubt would have gone viral.

Beyond Wick past the town's airport with signs for Bilbster and Sibster on the road, you might imagine a theme was developing. Up the road a bit there is a Nybster and Brabster and inland you might also find Lower Camster and Badlipster – consisting of a single farm house near to a place called Thuster. The *ster* is not from the Gaelic but from the Old Norse word for farm, which is a reminder from centuries before when the Caithness area was very much ruled by burley Norwegians. Happily, since the Treaty of Perth was signed in 1266, Norway considers Caithness to be very much a part of Scotland. However, given Norway is one of the richest countries in the world with enviable public services, and has one of the most developed and equal democracies that can frequently be found near to or at the top of those lists that occasionally do the rounds about happiness and general all-round spiffiness, there are many in Scotland who'd welcome Norwegian rule again.

In terms of the mainland, Wick is definitely in the north, but in terms of territory we were still a long way short of the north of Scotland in its truest sense. We've already mentioned Skaw, Scotland's most northerly settlement, but Out Stack (or Ootsta) represents the most northerly point. It's an uninhabited rock about two miles north of Unst in the Shetland Isles and still 180 odd miles north and little bit east of Wick. Be that as it may, with place names post-fixed with Old Norse language, the hard-to-explain and possibly subjective sense of remoteness, there was a different feel to the area. Continuing on to John O'Groats, we turned right (staying on the A99) at a small village called Reiss, then past the tiny settlements of Westerloch, Keiss, Nybster, Freswick and Everley – the road was straight with only occasional deviations. The landscape was flat, offering long views in all directions; neat fields gave way to wilder countryside clad in heather and evidence of peat cutting activity. With a final gasp of cultivated farmland and a greater concentration of the bungalow-and-out-building combo, we arrived at the village of John O'Groats.

Villages in the north of Scotland are often not the nucleated settlements we're used to. The abundance of space must encourage settlers to spread out, building their little bungalows hundreds of metres away from the nearest neighbours, and so it is with John O'Groats. There is a village centre with a post office and shop with petrol pumps out front, a hotel and small fire station surrounded by modest houses – the John O'Groats known to most is a bit further on past the village itself. As we approached, it was plain to see money had been spent – the hotel had been restored and a colourful Norse-style wing added. The shopping area was also looking a lot more attractive, and all in, it looked immeasurably better than it had on previous visits. We parked our recalcitrant minibus and set out to explore the area.

The most recognisable feature is the well known John O'Groats signpost. The arrows and destinations change dependant on when you're visiting, and on this occasion it was Orkney and Shetland, Land's End, New York, and Edinburgh. It was late on Tuesday afternoon and only the most hard-bitten shop owners had their doors open. Having a group of youths turn up must present proprietors with conflicting views – on the one hand it might be good for business but on the other, if they're all on the rob... Since our crowd don't go on the rob, it was all good news, although I'm not sure anyone bought anything, right enough. The allure of a key fob explaining what your clan name means and a sample of your clan tartan with your actual name on it (in case you forget) has limited effect. Tea towels with maps of Scottish distilleries, words to 'Flower of Scotland' or the insects of Scotland printed there-on similarly are of narrow attraction. The tourist shop can be an odd place if you're not a tourist. The range of goods on sale could be seen as a portrait of the country – sometimes the portrait is subtle and nuanced, but sometimes it's been scrawled by a chimp with a jumbo crayon. It's as if all the most popular Scottish stereotypes have crashed into the branding department of a marketing firm. At its most crass (and there was a fair bit of it at John O'Groats) it's a focus group driven exercise. Some twat in a roll-neck sweater and cords haranguing a group of people pulled off a street hundreds of miles from Scotland shouts, 'COME ON FOLKS, WHAT SAYS 'SCOTLAND' TO YOU?' and in a panic they blurt out the usual suspects: highland cows, shortbread, tartan, midges, tweed jumpers, bagpipes, kilts, whisky and so on. Someone else, possibly in another department which might be called Product Randomisation, takes all those things and marries them up to a disparate list of every day items. The result is key rings to remind you what your name is, tea towels to remind you what rosemary or thyme look like, knitted Scottie dogs to cover the spare bog roll in the smallest room, and 'locally made' tablet whose locally made credentials are confirmed by the image of a tiny highland dancer on the packaging.

What they've done with John O'Groats is great; the area looks about a million times better than it did, especially the old hotel. It's easy to mock the tourism industry, but the new shops there also showcased the kind of high quality food and drink that Scotland is becoming well known for, and in the background an eco-friendly holiday village is a testament to Scotland's intent in the world. I'm not sure what the young folk made of the place, but I was gratified to discover the tablet I'd bought was well past its sell by date – for some that might be cause for complaint, but to me it showed John O'Groats hadn't become one of those flavour-free commercial machines where everything is shiny and perfect.

Equally, the mould on the tablet may have affected my ability to reason.

Although it is said often, we may as well say it again: John O'Groats isn't the most northerly point on the Scottish mainland, that accolade goes to Easter Point on Dunnet head to the west. Leaving John O'Groats, all eyes were peeled for a suitable campsite. We had an idea we might camp at Dunnet Head itself if we could find a decent spot, but we had also talked about a place called Brough Bay. This sheltered cove sits in the eastern crook of the Dunnet Head peninsula and if you only need space for one or two tents, it's a viable site. However, it was very quickly becoming apparent that embarking on a tour without planning accommodation or scoping out suitable campsites doesn't really add to the adventure – it just leaves you frantically pecking away at smart phones searching for somewhere to stay, usually as the sun disappears beneath the horizon. Pitching a tent in the dark, not knowing what's over that wall or behind this hedge or possibly in the same field might mean adventure to some, but if you're travelling with young people who are still adored by their parents, a cavalier attitude to camping arrangements might be frowned upon.

A friend and I found Brough Bay on a motor cycle tour a year or two before. We parked our bikes and pitched our tent, and since the hour was late and the weather wet we went straight to bed. At some point during the night, over and above the sucking and swirling noise the waves made as the tide ebbed and flowed, other far more disturbing noises reached our ears – someone was obviously being murdered out to sea. It was a loud choking sob that cut off abruptly only to start again anew from a different direction with a different tone. We lay for quite some time pretending not to be worried until a particularly gut-churning shriek shattered our fake nonchalance and propelled us both from our sleeping bags. If you are being chased by a serial killer, the absolute worst place to take shelter is a hike tent; they are – albeit not deliberately – designed to impede your safety. If a horde of zombies decide to eat your brain, not only are the walls paper thin but by entering, you've essentially corralled yourself while those chasing (the walking dead or otherwise) could come unseen from any direction. If it's dark, switching a torch on makes it even worse because everything you do (and I do mean everything) is projected onto the wall behind in stark detailed relief. Truly, emerging of a morning wearing pants on your head with your trousers on back to front, although embarrassing, is the least of your worries if you feel certain murder is being committed just outside your tent.

Eventually though, we realised it was seals doing whatever it is seals do through the night – choking and drowning people to death it seemed to us. In the morning – by which I mean in the middle of night because the bright June sunlight woke us at 5am – we emerged gingerly from our tent to a view that made us forget completely just how early it was. Gone was the darkness, the wind, rain and blood curdling screams. Here in bright sunshine was Brough Bay with its rocky cliffs and sheer-sided islet set perfectly in its centre. We'd pitched our tent in front of some old lighthouse service buildings, and out in the broad bay seals were sunning themselves on the long slipway while others of a more curious nature had come nearer to find out what we were having for breakfast – or to find out if we were worth murdering.

The road down to the bay is precipitous and steep, so we stopped our borrowed minibus at the top and peered down dubiously (as the lights on the dashboard rippled and flashed). We decided not to chance it, so instead executed a seventy-two-point turn and made for Dunnet Head.

Dunnet Head protrudes three miles toward the Island of Hoy (second largest of the Orkney Isles). From it you can see east back to Duncansby Head (the most north easterly point on the Scottish mainland) and to the west toward the burgh of Thurso and a good bit beyond. The cliffs plunge 300ft to the sea, which at times can be so energetic stones thrown up by waves can break the windows of the Stevenson-built lighthouse there. Most of the land on the Dunnet peninsula is given over to rough grazing and peat cutting, but it's also pock-marked with small lochs: St John's Loch at the base (but technically not on the peninsula), the tiny Black Loch in the west, while in the east there is the equally-as-small Courtfall Loch, and to the north Loch Burifa, Loch Long and Loch of the Easter Head. If military history fascinates, there is much to look at: fortifications built to protect the naval base at Scapa Flow, and a Chain Home Low Station (an early warning radar system used during the Second World War). RAF Bomber Command operated a GEE navigation system from 1942 – using radio signal triangulation to locate planes, it was accurate to a few hundred metres as far away as 350 miles. Burifa Hill on Dunnet Head was home to the master station for the northern array. The name 'GEE' isn't an acronym, it's the phonetic representation of the letter G. The system was so called because the time delay between radio waves being transmitted, reflected by a plane, then picked up again, was measured then plotted onto a grid laid over a map. GEE refers to the letter G in the word grid. The person in charge of pithy/interesting names for top secret installations must have been on leave that day). During WW2 there was also an artillery range. More recently, the Royal Observer Corps (ROC) had an observation bunker there during the cold war; it closed with most other ROC posts in 1991 with the fall of the Communist Bloc. You might assume the Royal Observer Corps was fully staffed by one or other of the armed forces but on further reading, it turns out it was a civil defence concern staffed by enthusiastic volunteers. The ROC posts were not easy places to work in – sunken rooms with space for three people. From above, a hatch, a ventilation shaft and a panel holding some instrumentation were the only evidence of a ROC bunker, in fact, you may have seen them and not realised what they were. After a nuclear attack, ROC personnel (assuming they hadn't been baked alive) would man their posts and take measurements for between 7 and 21 days, locating ground zero blast points, measuring wind direction and radiation, and reporting it all back to headquarters. Fortunately, such measurements were never needed in reality.

Dunnet Head is wind swept even when it's not that windy. It feels remote (because it is) and with the abandoned buildings and heavy concrete foundations of buildings long since removed – the nature of which is obscure – there is a desolate feel to the place. We poked around for a while looking for a place to camp but decided eventually that it was just a little bit too exposed. The weather forecast wasn't overly bad but there was nowhere to camp that offered any shelter if the wind did get up, and we got the impression that if it did get windy, it would be very windy indeed.

On the road past Dunnet Head to Thurso, we were now firmly in search mode for a campsite. It was our intention to camp as much as possible while having one or two nights indoors to recuperate, plus our budget didn't really allow for indoor accommodation every night. Dunnet Head and Thurso might be remote but they're far from deserted and it was proving difficult to find a suitable spot to pitch tents. Wild camping presents issues if you're not truly in the wild, for example, where can one reasonably (being indelicate for a moment) go for a poo? Without getting into the nitty gritty, it's a bit of a problem if you're never more than 100metres (say) from the nearest dwelling, not to mention finding isolation from the people you're travelling with. I mean, you could wander off, find what from every angle looks like a suitably private spot, only to find you are evacuating your bowels onto some poor unsuspecting soul's herbaceous border. These are the issues you don't read about in Five Go off to Camp; it's all yummy eggs and scrumptious ham from the farmhouse nearby. There's no mention of the brave bunch unknowingly defecating in the farmer's wife's vegetable patch – even Timmy the dog seemed to avoid that faux pas.

The point is – and you can accuse us of not being hardy enough if you like – toilets are something of a prerequisite. Why be uncomfortable if you don't have to?

It got to the point where we had a choice between travelling further beyond Thurso (pretty much the last town on the north coast of any size) not knowing if we'd find an open and accommodating campsite, or returning to the town to find hostel space. If we couldn't manage that, the only other option was to play the Scout card and try to find space in a community or Scout hall. For the nights ahead, the leader team all agreed we should probably try to organise accommodation in the morning for the following nights. The young folk didn't seem to be bothered though, we told them we might end up camping on a central reservation on the outskirts of town, but they appeared to be drunk on a heady mix of fresh air and strawberry laces.

If you're visiting a town for a short period of time and mildly concern about where you are going to stay, it's hard not to form certain – possibly unfair – opinions of that town. Thurso might be really nice, but on a dull Tuesday evening with the night drawing in, driving round it's frustrating grid of one-way roads (which is probably quite straightforward in daylight), I couldn't claim to be a fan. We were looking for Sandra's. Contrary to what the name suggests, not a sauna or a gentleman's club, but Sandra's Backpacker hostel. We knew it existed because the internet said so; however, we first couldn't find the street it was on and when we eventually did, we couldn't find Sandra. I have a love/hate relationship with hostels. It's not one or the other as such, it's both feelings at the same time; I love to hate them. It's a form of masochism – Fifty Shades of Bunk Beds. It's the petty rules, the stupid signs, the irrational pedantry – and that's just the folk running them. The customers are often slightly unhinged, a murderer on the run is probably on a budget – it stands to reason – so they're probably using hostels. We may as well get this out the way now: Sandra's TripAdvisor page is terrible – it's difficult to find other hostels on the website with reports that are more negative. But listen, I liked it, I really did, it was quirky and the owners couldn't have been more helpful. Its people's expectations that are wrong. It was £14.50 a night and reviewers are complaining about there not being any breakfast in the morning, or the odd stray hair on the mattress, or that the mattresses had no sheets. You don't get any of that for fifteen quid a night, you just don't. I've never stayed in a hostel where breakfast was included, but Sandra's had cereal available, bread and milk, and jam and butter. Admittedly, one did wonder what had been dipped in the butter or whether the cereal needed to be carbon dated but listen – at least they offered it. I'm now sounding defensive. Yes, in truth, Sandra's was an oddity, but for so little money you're going to get some quirks. For example, check-in happens in the chip shop-cum-takeaway establishment on the ground floor. You are then directed round the corner where an external iron staircase takes you to the first floor, which has rooms, toilets, laundry and a communal kitchen and diner where Wifi was available but moody. A second floor held more rooms.

It's not uncommon in remote areas for several businesses to operate out of the same premises. We've all seen the pictures of Irish pubs filled with craic, Guinness and groceries for sale, so why not a takeaway/hostel? I mean, it wasn't at the cutting edge in terms of catering equipment and while it looked a wee bit greasy around the edges, I've had late night pizzas out of far grubbier establishments. The people seemed fine, and the owner found space for us – he knew we couldn't put the young folk in a room with anyone else (child safety – some things you always take seriously). Our young people got two rooms on the second floor while we got a room on the first. The bed situation was quirky with Leaders Number Two and Three having to share the lower double bunk while I had to exercise my inner mountain goat to get to the top single bunk (some responders on TripAdvisor *really* didn't like that arrangement). There was an en suite shower of sorts, although it would have been just as effective to have someone flick water at you out of a bowl, and a TV in the corner, which wouldn't turn on. We soon realised we needed a key to where our Explorers would be sleeping, as the door to their rooms had locks and were behind another solid outer door that also locked on closing. More than one respondent on TripAdvisor pointed out the fire risk – if (for example) they succumbed to smoke inhalation because someone forgot to turn off a chip fryer downstairs, rescuers would have to kick down many doors after climbing that external metal staircase as flames licked at their feet. I'd be lying if I said the thought hadn't crossed my mind.

Since most people assume buildings won't spontaneously combust, our main concern was noise – a heard of adolescents on the move in any building isn't subtle in terms of noise. If the sensors were still present at that ROC post on Dunnet Head, civil defence volunteers could have identified Sandra's as a potential ground zero blast point that Tuesday night, so we secured more keys.

After opening and closing all the cupboards and drawers in our rooms (which as a species, is something we just seem to do) we congregated in the communal kitchen-cum-dining area on the first floor. This was a hostel in the classic style, all wood panelling with many international mementos hanging on the walls. Already in the room was a couple travelling around the north of Scotland in a hire car. We never found out their names, but that was the only information the fellow didn't attempt to impart during a very long, mostly one-sided conversation that occurred while his travelling companion sat quietly by with a beatific smile on her face – it's entirely possible she may have been drugged. Dinner for leaders was beef in black bean sauce served with rice – about a ton of it going by how much we decided to cook. I remember throwing out a lot of rice and when I say a lot, I mean a cubic foot of it. The kids had pasta in tomato sauce heavily augmented with slices of the smoked plastic horseshoe-shaped sausage they bought that morning. I'd like to see how these sausages are made. They can't be extruded in the way ordinary sausages are – you know what I mean, a big long tube of sausage skin, slipped onto a stainless steel teat from which sausage meat squirts in a satisfying stream. These 'smoked pork' horseshoes must be grown or moulded somehow, but when I try to imagine it, my mind draws a complete blank – we should probably revisit this later on. It was proving to be a popular staple among the young folk – a definite go-to meat substitute in many dinners throughout the week. Dinner that night was a late affair, so it was after eight before we sat down to eat and closer to nine by the time we'd tidied up. Although the hostel was full that night, we only saw the boring couple, as no other internees showed face in the communal area.

The dining room at Sandra's Backpackers

After dinner we colonised the communal space to play cards while a DVD ran in the background – in fact, it might have been a VHS tape such was the nature of the place. This was partly out of a sense of camaraderie between Leaders and Explorers but also for safety – although the minibus had another Scout Group's name on the side, I'd given my real name when we booked in. We didn't want the young people having a wild party and trashing the place if we went to the pub.

The building in which Sandra's operates needs to be oiled – all of it. It was without doubt one of the noisiest places I've ever spent a night in. Turning over in bed in one corner of the building sent a wave front of squeaks and groans to the opposite corner, whilst flushing the toilet set free a cacophony of animal-like hoots and brays. There is a saying: each time you light a cigarette from a candle, a sailor dies at sea – well, every time you flush a bog at Sandra's, a very unhappy cat is slooshed through the plumbing to die at sea.

Digressing for a moment, that saying about lighting cigarettes from candles and sailors dying, I read that in a book some time ago and thought I'd look up its history. By which I mean, I thought I'd Google it and only read the top two returns – I am nothing if not average. The first suggestion is from an online magazine site called *Stars & Stripes* (www.stripes.com). One of their correspondents was travelling in Europe back in 2007; he lit a cigarette from a candle in a pub and it set local fingers wagging. Apparently, during lean months when the fish weren't biting, fishermen used to supplement their income by making matches, ergo, if you lit a cigarette from a candle, you wouldn't be using a match so potentially doing a fisherman an economic mischief. The second entry is from the blog of a travelling street musician known as The Dead Sea Captain (on Blogspot at time of writing if you're interested).

The first paragraph starts:

"When you light your cigarette from a candle, a sailor dies at sea. That is a Polish superstition. I was sitting in De Graal yesterday and overheard it. First I got to tell you about De Graal. Out of all the Coffee Shop culture in Amsterdam, De Graal is by far the most like I

imagined a coffee shop would be in my dreams. It is like going into a friend's house. Comfy chairs all around, fish tanks, a dancing chameleon who eats grass hoppers, a recording studio and the best coffee and cheapest weed in town!"

Sadly, 'The Dead Sea Captain' must have smoked too much weed because he forgot to return to the 'Polish superstition' deciding instead to embark upon a self-absorbed monologue:

"Sometimes I feel incredibly low and challenged by the uncertainty of my lifestyle."

He goes on at length in the same vein to which I'd suggest: dry your eyes pal, at least you're not an out of work Polish fisherman working in a matchstick factory. Imagine if we lived in a society that informed itself solely on the first two returns of a Google search, wouldn't that be awful, or maybe we already do? Also, I can't believe I read that guy's self-involved mutterings.

The night at Sandra's (once things had settled down) was passable, although a little bit noisy; the takeaway downstairs was open till late and seemed to be a favourite of taxi drivers who sat outside and guzzled food and revved engines. At around 3am, the minibus alarm went off causing me to leap from my eyrie on the top bunk, crushing Leader Number Three's ribs in the process. We'd been in the habit of feeding the skinniest child in through a window to lock the side door from the inside, but it was by no means a foolproof process. I peered anxiously out the window but nothing moved on the mean streets of Thurso. I strained my ears but couldn't hear anything suspicious over the gasping whoops Leader Number Three was making in order to get his breath back. I returned to bed, standing on Leader Number Two's face for good measure.

Day Five – Thurso to Achiltibuie and Altandhu

Sandra's Backpackers, I was recently told the takeaway part of the business had closed.

Day five dawned bright and sunny if a little chilly. Failing to learn from the night's injuries, Leaders Number Two and Three still slumbered but, since daylight streamed through the threadbare curtains, I manage to descend with enough grace to avoid further injury. People were on the move in the building, although it was hard to tell if the young people were among them. I listened carefully but decided despite the manifold shrieks and feline wailing coming from the walls, none of it seemed loud enough.

Turning the shower on had no appreciable effects; a fat languorous drip appeared from the lowermost hole but couldn't find the enthusiasm to detach itself. Instead I brushed my teeth and pulled my hair into something other than the mess it had become overnight. I found all the keys I needed to access the rooms the young people occupied and made my way up the metal stairs attached to the outside of the building. The two dorms the kids were allocated sat side by side in their own small hallway. Unfortunately, none of the keys seemed to open the outer door but eventually, after having tried all of them at least twice, I managed to gain access. I loudly cleared my throat and knocked on the first door. I needn't have bothered because as there was no response, I ended up unlocking this door only after trying each key twice. As I stepped gingerly into the room, a familiar odour made its way up my nostrils, not quite eye watering as such but unpleasant nonetheless. Vague forms moved on the bunks like oversized multicoloured larvae from an alien planet, possibly known to space-farers as 'the one that smells a bit mulchy'. A leg snaked out from a sleeping bag to hang limply in front of a nose that had tentatively appeared on the bunk beneath, only to be withdrawn in disgust. I pulled the curtains open to let light flood into the room and watched as young people recoiled in horror to the backs of bunk beds like vampires retreating to the shadows. I went to the other room, but couldn't unlock the door at all, so just waited for someone to open it from the inside. The en suite shower was in use and the curtains (and window) already opened. Compared to the other room it smelled like a summer meadow. I gave the usual morning messages about packing up, breakfast and leaving the rooms tidy and returned to do exactly that in my own room.

A lot of the other hostel detainees had already packed up and left, but the man and his still distant-looking partner were drinking tea in the dining room. As Explorers got organised upstairs, we set about getting breakfast organised and in between times took advantage of the fractious Wifi to hunt for a suitable campsite for the coming night. We had an idea we might camp at a place called Ardmair just north of Ullapool, but we'd since learned it was closed for the winter. As bacon and square sausage fried, I pecked away at my phone looking for an alternative, eventually finding a campsite that was open at a place called Altandhu near to Achiltibuie. Named Port A Bhaigh Campsite, it looked to be decent enough as it came complete with a brand new, spacious toilet block with showers and washing up area and, most importantly, the Am Fuaran Bar right over the road. I'm not saying that's what made us choose it. That there was a pub nearby – truthfully – was a happy coincidence. Not many campsites remain open past the beginning of October and while there are a lot more wild spaces down the west coast of Scotland, we didn't want to spend hours hunting around for a suitable spot. We looked for wild campsites (no really, we did) but people tend not to put it about if they find an idyllic camping spot complete with sandy beach offering shelter from the wind and copious amounts of firewood – I'd probably keep it to myself too.

Young people began to appear, fresh-faced and damp-haired from the en suite showers that seemed to work a lot better than ours. As we described where we'd be camping that night – our most remote overnight spot to date – Ally, who would be leaving us a day early to go on holiday with his family, declared that it was very near to where they'd be spending the following week. It turns out our campsite at Altandhu was less than half a mile away from the cottage his parents had rented.

As rolls stuffed with bacon, square sausage and the odd fried egg were consumed, the owners came into the kitchen to ask how we slept and what our plans were. Glossing over how we slept, we talked about our route and asked after a supermarket so we could resupply for the following two days or so. It's good to know that Thurso is home to the last supermarket on the north coast until Ullapool way down on the west coast. There are plenty of small independent shops, many of which the young folk cleaned out of Irn Bru and Mars Bars. Sometimes though, they don't hold enough stock to feed a dozen hungry mouths over and above what they'd normally keep for local needs. On trips in the past, we've been the recipients of angry glares as we've commandeered all the rolls or bacon or wine in a small local shop – sometimes it's best just to buy it from the man, so to speak.

I would like to reiterate that the owners of the hostel couldn't have been more accommodating. Yes, it was a bit grubby and none of us took advantage of the timeless cereal or the complementary bread and butter, but I think the owners took our request for information as an opportunity to get rid of food left by previous customers: three loaves of generic 'value' bread, several pints of full fat milk, enough rice to more than replace the cubic foot we threw out the night before and, somewhat randomly, a box of couscous. We are nothing if not polite so accepted these gifts with suitable levels of gratitude matched by comparable levels of confusion about what you're supposed to do with couscous.

Normal rules for Scout camp apply: you leave a campsite in pristine condition, even if you didn't find it that way. However, since none of us were electricians, plumbers or builders, it wasn't possible to do this at Sandra's Backpacker Hostel. But you know what, if they fixed all that stuff, getting rid of the squeaky floors, the tempestuous plumbing and the fossilised cornflakes, it would be a deeply uninteresting place to stay. Go and have a look on TripAdvisor and come back and tell me you weren't just a little pleased that the wasp chewing 'Anna C' couldn't figure out how the keys worked so had a horrible time, or that 'Anon866' was horrified that the breakfast provided (bearing in mind the low tariff) was of such low quality he'd never return (ever), or 'Kenny M' who was so scandalised by the low standards he suggested you stay away 'for your own health'. Those poor fragile souls rushing around shrieking and tearing their hair out because they found a suspiciously curly hair on a mattress or were handed towels that were grey – I mean to say, for £15 a night, the humanity.

There are some truly bad reviews for Sandra's on TripAdvisor, but all I can say is our experience was fine; it was cheap and cheerful and our hosts couldn't have been more helpful. Some TripAdvisor contributors don't seem to understand its B&Bs and hotels that offer cooked breakfasts, not hostels. Sandra's is the first I've ever stayed in that went beyond complimentary tea and coffee. Equally, for £15 a night, you've got to accept the odd hair (that isn't yours) into your life. It's only for one night and it's not like it'll get you pregnant.

The sunlight cast Thurso in a more attractive light, certainly more so than the previous evening. We repacked the van, being careful to ensure the couscous was suitably stored, and made our way back the way we had come the night before in order to go to the superstore on the eastern outskirts of the town. The next two days and nights would see us travel through the most remote parts of the Scottish mainland: from Thurso to Durness, then south to Altandhu, then to Ullapool and on to the Corrieshalloch Gorge where we'd veer westwards toward Gruinard, Aultbea and Gairloch. At Gairloch, we'd start zigzagging to Kinlochewe, pass through Torridon to Sheildaig, then to Strathcarron and Stromeferry, eventually ending up two nights later at Kyle of Lochalsh wondering if we should try to find somewhere on Skye to stay that night. Total distance travelled would be in the region of 298 miles, not including the inevitable detours, and it would all start from the car park of Thurso's branch of Tesco.

The young people seemed to be leaving behind their shop-based option paralysis. Sure, they still loaded up with Haribo, Flying Saucers and those luminous 'energy' drinks that are so popular with young people (and despised by parents), but their main meal choice was becoming more wholesome and we made sure to be on hand to help with weights and amounts. We talked about it the night before at Sandra's and suggested again that it was probably better to have too much than too little. During our weekly Explorer meetings, we occasionally cook, anything from simple pancakes to setting a budget for a main course of their choice, which they'd prepare and present in a Master Chef style. (Which never works by the way, the food they prepare always looks like it's been hit with a shovel.) We've also experimented with boil-in-the-bag food (it's surprising what you can boil in a sandwich bag, although the results aren't always attractive) and with a thing called chocolate mug cake. While doing so, we've discovered it doesn't matter what we cook it will probably be consumed by someone; Harry for example enjoys cornflakes on a roll with brown sauce and, for the short time he's been with us, we've learned that Explorer Andrew will eat anything. Take the chocolate mug cake for example; the idea is you scale down all the ingredients you'd normally use to bake a chocolate cake, put them in a mug, mix them up, then zap the whole thing in a microwave. What comes out is a cross between a small chocolate cake and the foam you find in cushions. It's not completely inedible, it's just horrible; we think Andrew knew this but doggedly ate his mug cake anyway. He either has a pathological fear of food waste or his parents aren't feeding him – we suspect the former because we know his parents are decent people.

Sadly our Explorers hadn't left behind their indestructible relationship with the Mattesson's Smoked Pork Sausage, but, as is often reported on trite motivational posters: Why reach for the Finest Organic Apple and Cranberry Banger in the sky, when there's a Mattesson's Smoked Pork Sausage on the moon? I may have paraphrased somewhat.

Thurso is an attractive town in daylight, and it's also the most northerly town on the Scottish mainland and a stop off point for those travelling to Orkney via the port of Scrabster a few miles away. It's also the closest town to the Dounreay Nuclear Complex, although it no longer generates power. All three of its reactors have been shut down, the last one in 1994, but it's still so dangerous a high number of specialist staff are required to stop it from blowing up, melting down or otherwise irradiating the north coast and the nearby town of Thurso. Also on site is the Vulcan Naval Reactor Test Establishment (formerly just HMS Vulcan). It was here (until 2015 anyway) they designed nuclear power plants to power Royal Navy submarines. Interestingly, the site is operated for the Royal Navy by Rolls Royce from their offices in Derby some 550 miles to the south – make of that what you will.

In any case, all of that means Thurso enjoys the spoils of having specialist industry on its doorstep, so it's not a complete ghost town.

It is true to say it doesn't have world class attractions like Wick's shortest street in the world, but it has the River Thurso, which runs through the town, and is so called to honour the Norse god Thor, who according to *Hello! Magazine*, used to holiday in Thurso with his family. It is not known if they stayed at Sandra's Backpackers Hostel; however, if they did, it was probably the same cornflakes in the Tupperware box then as when we visited – Thor probably needed his hammer to dislodge them from the container.

The road west out of Thurso is similar to the road in from the east, with views toward Scrabster and the ferry to Stromness and the Orkney Isles. After that, it's back to small fields and the occasional bungalow-with-outbuildings as you leave Thurso Bay behind. Through the picturesque village of Bridge of Forss and past Lybster farm, the road veers to the left where an arrow straight military road then takes you past Dounreay Power Station. You can easily see the 139ft sphere that held the Dounreay Fast Reactor. It was the first of its kind to provide electricity to homes in 1962, and although it closed down in 1977, decommissioning is ongoing. According to the Dounreay Site Restoration website, they spent some time figuring out what else the sphere could be used for, but since it is still slightly radioactive, it was decided that it would be dismantled as part of the wider decommissioning process. I for one think Mattesson's are missing trick here. There isn't much that is natural about their smoked pork sausage anyway and I'm sure the background radioactivity could be marketed as a safety feature, say, to keep the microbes at bay. Equally, in terms of climate change, since your sausage would arrive already slightly warm, there could be net savings on carbon emissions from electricity generation.

They can have that one for free.

On past the village of Reay and Sandside Beach, you can't really see it from the road, but it has been in the news. Situated 3 km from Dounreay itself, it's also known as Nuclear Beach. In 1984 a particle was detected; however, it's difficult to know what that really means. I mean, was it a grain-of-sand-sized particle, something as big as a tennis ball or an actual particle? In fact, hundreds of *particles* have been found there and the site is now monitored on a regular basis. Referring again to the Dounreay Site Restoration website, it turns out Sandside isn't the only Nuclear Beach in the area; particles have also been found at Murkle 18 km away. Reading a little further in to it, in 1977 an underground explosion occurred that caused thousands of radioactive particles to be flushed into the sea, many of which now regularly wash up on local beaches. Apparently, one of these particles was described thusly by the Dounreay Particles Advisory Group:

"On 15th December 2006, during a survey for radioactive particles at Sandside beach, an object was discovered, towards the eastern end of the beach, which was not the same as the particles typically found on the beach. The object, which was detected due to the presence of Caesium-137, was lying in seaweed close to the water's

edge. The object is dark coloured and the outside surface appears to (sic) the object's approximate dimensions are 8 inches long by 3 inches wide and 1 inch thick."

So not a 'particle' as we might understand it, and 'presence of Caesium-137' might also be code for slightly glowing. They also kept the details of the explosion quiet (so to speak) until 1996 – but fear not, Rolls Royce staff at the Derby office were entirely unharmed.

After the village of Reay and Sandside Beach (about which there are glowing reports, nuclear particles notwithstanding) the landscape does change, with small arable farmland giving way to wild grazing scarred by peat cutting, and the road narrows considerably – you know you're in the country side when you start seeing passing places on the road.

By this time we'd come to terms with the young folks not being interested in what we were calling 'scenery' and since from that point forward 'scenery' was going to be the main distraction, we wondered how they would manage. In hindsight, we probably wouldn't do a road trip quite like this again. Instead, we might base ourselves in one place and travel around to look at interesting things. The Explorers, however, still seemed to be enjoying themselves. It was still something of an adventure being away with friends, and many hadn't been north of Inverness before, but it was becoming clear that spending so much time in the minibus was beginning to tell. Since they'd finished the walking phase back in Fort Augustus, the routine now was we'd travel in the van, stop occasionally here and there and explore a bit, then all pile back into the minibus and move on to the next interesting looking thing on our route. As we travelled, the leader team would sit up front and the young folk would have the run of the rearmost section behind the minibus's bench seat. Every now and again we'd dip into the chat only to withdraw in confusion. We'd ask Michael what they were talking about and he'd give an airy response which included words like 'Dr Who', 'GoT' or 'strawberry laces' – Lewis and I would then return to the scenery.

Our fellow travellers sometimes seemed so far away…

In between stops, attentions in the back of the van didn't seem to stray outside very often. I suppose in most groups you get strong characters who like to be the focus of attention, and ours wasn't any different. We've had many groups of friends pass through our hands (as it were), but this group is most memorable for their ability to keep themselves occupied with minimal external input.

It helps that they all know each other outside of Scouts. During that week, we didn't hear any angry words between the young folk and from my own point of view (as a very reluctant disciplinarian) not once did I have to beat the crap out of anyone (I'm joking, we haven't been able to do that since the 1980's). Within the group, there was the capacity to be irritated and to be irritating, but it never escalated beyond a reproachful look or a good-natured but uncompromising request to stop being a knob. Even though they all seemed happy – the chatter rarely abated – I was worried that at times they were perhaps a bit bored.

Stocked up with supplies and Haribo for the next 48 hours, we travelled on with no new warning lights on the van's fascia. Our plans for the day included stops at Bettyhill (to give the shopkeeper a fright), cavorting on the beach at Rispond, a visit to Smoo Cave at Durness and, although we didn't know at that point, a visit to Balnakeil Craft Village just beyond Durness.

The next significant settlement on the A836 was Melvich and by significant, I mean the usual bungalows-with-outbuildings, just a bit more bunched up than usual. If you look at the area around Melvich and Portskerra on Google Earth, you can see evidence of the old 'run rig' method of farming. This is often mistaken for modern ploughing or grass cutting, and a good example of this can be seen if you look at aerial photography of The Braid Hills Golf Club in Edinburgh. You can more easily tell the neat strips left by grass cutting from the much older evidence of rig farming. It's difficult to find information on the topic because the internet insists on telling you about Runrig, the popular Scottish band, as opposed to the popular 18th century Scottish 'rig-a-rendal' system of farming. In any case, back in the day, land would be segregated into manageable chunks (called touns or townships) for communal farming. An area for grazing would be set aside accessible to all with animals, while the 'in-bye' (areas of farmland suitable for arable food production) would be separated into narrow strips called 'rigs', which in turn would be separated by 'runs' of fallow ground (for the purposes of drainage, wildlife and keeping the next door neighbours from encroaching on your rig).

Melvich and Portskerra enjoy winsome views across the River Halladale where it meets Melvich Bay at Bighouse Lodge, part of the Sutherland Estates (which we've already talked about) since 1829. Interestingly, Bighouse was one of many homes of Clan Mackay, who fought alongside forces loyal to the English monarch during the Jacobite risings. At the clan's peak they controlled territory from Reay to Durness and Cape Wrath, and as far south as the Assynt Peninsula. Looking into the activities of the Mackay Clan over the years, it's easier to say who they haven't fought than try to keep track of who they have. One thing that caught my eye was, after the Battle of Harpsdale in 1426, the clan chief Angus Du Mackay and his son trashed much of Caithness. The inhabitants were obviously a bit miffed and got together to say so, which led to even further bloodshed. So much so that James I travelled to Inverness intent on getting to grips with the ornery Mackays. Bravely and honourably, Angus Du Mackay prostrated himself before the king's mercy and pledged his son as a guarantee of future good behaviour. Neil (Angus Du's understandably pissed-off son) was carted off and imprisoned on the Bass Rock in the Firth of Forth not a million miles away from where our Explorer group is from. King James also commended Angus Du Mackay on his choice of name for his house on Melvich Bay, for it was indeed a big house.

I made that up, Bighouse as it stands today wasn't built until 1765, and up until then it was known variously as Small Plot, Bijou Fort and Good Sized Cottage. Seriously though, Bighouse Lodge is now a posh hotel offering fishing, stalking and shooting. If you are a vegetarian, an animal rights activist or an opponent of those who like to blast away at defenceless quadrupeds and startled winged creatures, I suggest you don't visit the Bighouse Lodge website and look at their fishing, stalking and shooting sections.

We trundled on in our minibus past tiny settlements: Baligill, Strathy, Aultiphurst, Lednagullin and Armadale. These ranged from being single farmhouses to half a dozen crofts lining the coast – or just a sign with nothing to see at all. Eventually we got to the winsomely named Bettyhill. I should say, ever since stopping in Bettyhill a number of years ago on a motor cycle tour, I fell in love with the place. Let me tell you why: there is a version of the Scottish accent made famous by Mel Gibson's portrayal of William Wallace in the historically accurate film *Braveheart*. (I'm joking, it's not historically accurate, it's rather a lot of arse gravy.) Even so, the accents – including those coming from Scottish actors – were something to behold if you're Scottish. I'm not precious about it, I think it's hilarious – probably in the same way my South African accent is hilarious. (Although it has been said when I do my 'Nelson Mandela' it's like he's in the room.) In any case, look at the places around Bettyhill and say their names in your broadest Brigadoon Scots – go on, its good fun, gie it some welly. Kirtomy – get the 'r' rolling and emphasise the 'om'; Achnabourin – emphasise the 'Ach', it should sound as if you have hair from a stranger stuck in your throat, go for it, and really spit that third syllable out; and finally, Achargary – go on, pretend you're an outboard motor and someone just put you in reverse.

Now say Bettyhill.

Doesn't really work, does it? You can say it in as broad a Scots accent you can muster – it still won't feel right. There's a reason for its incongruity and it'll probably make you roll your eyes. Strathnaver Valley runs for 18 miles or so to the south of Bettyhill and formed part of the Sutherland Estates – you may be able to guess where this is going. The valley was well populated until it was cleared between 1811 and 1821 by Patrick Sellar, factor of the Sutherland estates of whom we've heard previously. As many as 15,000 people were forcibly moved, some to the new settlement of Bettyhill – named after the Countess of Sutherland, Elizabeth Sutherland Leveson-Gower, or Betty. Some accounts say it was unusual for a replacement village to be built for those cleared to the coast, others said that the Duchess, her factor and her auditor (a shithead called James Loch) had a reputation for cruelty. Remember, life wasn't particularly easy before the clearances took place. People lived a hand-to-mouth existence, but they weren't starving. That only happened after they were evicted and moved to infertile land on the coast and given little choice but to try to produce food in ways they weren't skilled or prepared for. In a letter to a pal in England, Betty commented at the time: 'Scotch people are of happier constitution and do not fatten like the larger breed of animals.' Putting the rank arrogance to one side for a moment, her comment does two things: it completely glosses over the effects of her cruel land reforms (that caused people to starve to death) and puts the tone of the village's name in some context – imagine having no choice but to live in a village named for the person who forced you off the land your family had farmed for generations and killed your friends and neighbours?

The 19th Countess of Sutherland was born in Leven Lodge in Edinburgh, which as far as I can tell was (and still is) located in

Portobello. There are places in Edinburgh where a countess named Elizabeth would never be referred to as Betty, Portobello is not one of those places. I like to think the old bag took a little bit of her Portobello background up north and had it in mind when she christened Bettyhill, although it's a shame she didn't have any humility in mind when she condemned thousands to penury and death.

But listen, that was then and this is now. Bettyhill has a school with a swimming pool open to the public, there is the Strathnaver Museum – also known as the Mackay Museum - and an attractive beach at Torrisdale Bay, popular with surfers. There's also a café, a hotel and a couple of shops, one of which we piled into to restock our dwindling supplies of Skittles, Giant Buttons and energy drinks. It's an attractive place with old and new housing dotted in amongst tussocky hillocks and rocky crags, so much so that it is not possible to see the entire village from any one point. It's also quite remote – the kind of place where if you need new shoes but you want to try them on first, it means a day trip to town, and if you needed something a bit more specialist, a trip to Inverness wouldn't see you back in time for dinner.

The road out of Bettyhill turns south to follow the River Naver, through tiny single-dwelling hamlets – Achina, Invernaver, Leckfurrin and Achnabourin – which are marked on maps but not signposted on the road. Apropos of nothing other than it springs to mind, the bridge the road uses to span the River Naver just beyond Bettyhill is a solid early 20th century construction. I read that it's unusual because its plated girder parapets also carry the load, which means its sides are solid iron about four feet high. If you're crossing the bridge on a motorcycle and someone decides to film you from up the road, and if you stand up on the foot pegs, because the bridge's sides hide the bike you're riding perfectly, it looks like you're running very quickly across the bridge. I realise this is completely useless information but I think you would agree, it fits in nicely with this book so far.

The road meanders westward across moorland punctuated with rocky outcrops toward Tongue, eventually crossing the River Borgie. On past minor lochans with unpronounceable names such as Loch Tuirslighe and Loch Dubh Beul Na Faire to the north, and Clair-loch Mor and Loch Crocach to the south. I'm going to run out of superlatives quite quickly because this part of Scotland is a joy to behold, even the young people were taken aback by the vistas unfurling before them. As the road makes its way round the shoulder of the satisfyingly pointy Cnoc an Fhreiceadain, the full majesty of the Kyle of Tongue presents itself – it would induce the most indifferent observers to say something complimentary. The village of Tongue was also lovely in the sunshine with the bulk of Ben Loyal as a backdrop. The village boasts a couple of hotels, a shop and post office along with a primary school, which is handy information if you have pre-teen children and are planning to move there. It is a village in the classic sense, having a centre surrounded by houses on proper streets, as opposed to randomly placed bungalows and farmsteads which is the standard. The road takes a sharp turn and doubles back on itself where a causeway wafts travellers across the Kyle in safety. I say waft, we trundled – you don't waft anywhere in a Ford Transit Minibus, especially our particular minibus. Once across, there's more pleasing emptiness punctuated by occasional lochans, curious sheep and peat cuttings.

The road between the Kyle of Tongue and the next significant point of interest, Loch Eriboll, is much the same as the road between Bettyhill and the Kyle of Tongue: peat cutting, lochans and a whole lot of not much at all. The road eventually drops down into the settlement of Hope which sits at the northern tip of Loch Hope which has at its southern end Ben Hope, Scotland's most northerly Munro at 3041ft. Although Ben Hope isn't high on the list in terms of height (256th out of 282), sitting as it does in a relatively flat landscape, it looks impressively pointy in the distance.

If the view across the Kyle of Tongue was a poke in the ribs then catching sight of Loch Eriboll is a punch in the gob – even the surliest teenager (not that any of ours are) couldn't fail to be diverted by it. It's a sea loch, a deep gash running inland for eight miles or so, and within it there lies an island called Eilean Choraidh or Horse Island – so called because of the ancient race of sentient horses that used to rule there (it goes without saying I made that up). Loch Eriboll is still used as a deep water harbour and shelter for ships travelling around the dangerous Cape Wrath to the west and the Pentland Firth to the east. Small scale lime extraction took place from the surrounding landscape, much of which was processed in kilns which can be seen as you come round the road from the east at Ard Neakie – a rocky hillock of land out in the loch connected by what not an awful lot of people know is called a 'tombolo', a narrow spit of sand and shingle that connects a small island to the shore. I can't imagine where or when that knowledge might come in useful, but when it does, people will think you are very clever indeed. On Ard Neakie, travellers can see the old Heilam ferry house near to the lime kilns (all now derelict) which connected eastern villages with those on the west before the road was built. The whole place is just asking to be explored, but we didn't have time to stop.

The tombolo reaching out to Ard Neakie on Loch Eriboll

Loch Eriboll is the most sparsely populated area in Scotland (and the UK). Other than the 'village' of Eriboll, which consists of a couple of farmhouses and some trees, there's bugger all there. Not only that, but it's in the most remote part of mainland Scotland. I think the best way of putting it is to say once you've reached Loch Eriboll, it doesn't matter if you keep going or turn back, you'll still be going back to what many consider to be civilisation. Having said all that, it's been a busy place in the past; men of HMS Hood had their last shore leave at Portnancon on the western shore before the Battle of Denmark Strait. HMS Hood was sunk by shells from the Prinz Eugen and the Bismarck – of the 1418 men on board when she sank, only three survived. Horse Island was used as a representation of the battleship Tirpitz by the Fleet Air Arm for target practice, and thirty-three German U-boats surrendered in the loch thus spelling the end of the battle of the Atlantic. Even now, parts of the loch and shore are leased by the Ministry of Defence (MOD) for amphibious landing practice, and in 2011, one of the largest war games staged in recent years was based in the loch – so it has its livelier moments.

Normally you'd say a twenty-odd-mile dog-leg round a body of water would be a pain – where's the bridge? you might mutter to yourself. But the area around Loch Eriboll is captivating in its desolation. Rhianna who was always keen to take photographs used every opportunity to do so, whilst even the most apathetic passengers could be seen admiring the views out over the water. I mean, it would be nice to look at and spend time around here anyway, but its remote and untouched state lends it an almost other-worldly feel. I might even suggest that if you woke up in the area without knowing how you got there, you might think am I the only person alive or am I in a Scandinavian TV program featuring a detective in a chunky knit sweater about to be murdered?

It's very remote, so the solitude of the place makes you have odd thoughts.

Travelling back up the western shore takes you past Bronze Age remains: a 'souterrain' (a subterranean structure of indeterminate purpose) and a 'wheelhouse', also known as an 'Atlantic roundhouse', mostly because of its round shape. The more immature traveller can have his or her photo taken for their Facebook profile picture beside the place sign for the tiny community of Laid – I'm not saying we didn't stop, and I'm not saying we did, in fact, I'm not saying anything at all. Also on the western shore, those with an interest in ceramic art might be thrilled to know the celebrated artist Lotte Glob has a studio – I only know this because I saw it on an episode of Grand Designs. Lotte often scours the mountains in the area for materiel to include in her sculptures, and once finished she places them back out in the countryside in their new form to be enjoyed by anyone who finds them, which I think is a brilliant idea. It's just a shame there are so few people to find and appreciate them, although, if it was closer to what many call 'civilisation', some git would probably pinch them for their garden. Lotte used to have her studio at Balnakeil Craft Village just past Durness but more on that later.

Before we go on to explore the bright lights of Durness and its environs, I don't want anyone to think I'm ignoring the young people in this account. It's just that, as we travelled, it was difficult to hear or interact with anyone in the rearmost parts of the van. With the bench seat behind leaders given over to storage, the nearest young person was a good five feet away in a rattling and rumbling van. My attention was very much on the road, new lights as they appeared on the dashboard and the scenery as it presented itself, so since my attentive abilities aren't that broad to begin with, it didn't leave much for what was going on in the rear part of the minibus.

Suffice to say, they were all still there but on the off chance they were becoming dozy or listless behind the steamed up windows, we decided to stop for some fresh air at Rispond beach.

Making our way down to Rispond Beach

First of all, let's get the superlatives out of the way. It's a beach in the classic Scottish Highlands and Islands sense of the word; the water on the day we visited was a deep blue, and the azure sky was clear of clouds. All in all it was exactly what you would want from a beach in the north west of Scotland and because we were visiting out of season, we had it all to ourselves. The exemplary half mile crescent of white sand was merely being teased by the waves rolling in from the sea during our visit, but we could well imagine it being a good deal livelier in stormier circumstances. At its eastern end a small burn wends its way past hillocks and a ruined byre, whilst at the western edge, a huge sand dune begs the adventurous to leap from the top and roll down its steep face. I refrained, obviously, as it would be indecorous in the extreme, and I need to maintain a measure of aplomb because the young people look up to me, you see. Also, I probably wouldn't have made it to the top without having a heart attack – it's a fair-sized sand dune as these things go.

First aid skills still figure big at Scouts; we cover various techniques up to and including CPR. But, being reasonable, I don't think they'd appreciate me keeling over in their presence, except perhaps as an opportunity to go through my pockets... Of course, I'm joking, if I have a heart attack they are exactly the people I'd like to have around me at the time if only to see the looks on their faces when they realised I would require mouth-to-mouth ventilation. I dare say it'd be the last thing I'd ever see, but at least I'd being going out thoroughly entertained – my last words would be: 'Ha ha... the look on your fa– .'

We explored, clambered and cavorted until we could explore, clamber and cavort no more, then we returned to our van and made for Durness and Smoo Cave. But before we move on, let me tell you about Rispond Beach's Facebook page – it's part of a phenomenon (of which I am vaguely aware) of improbable things having Facebook pages. Rispond Beach's is not particularly active; it doesn't for example post pictures of what it's having for tea or of cats. There are half a dozen photos, one of which comes with the comment, 'Ej hvor er der pænt!', which Google Translate tells me is Danish and means, 'Fuck me, isn't this lovely!' I'm joking, according to Google Translate it means, 'Not where there nicely!' A young lady called Andrea Sofie Schendström answers, 'Ja! Desværre var det lige koldt nok til at bade – Ellers havde jeg taget en dukkert.' That roughly translates into, 'Yes! Unfortunately, it was just cold enough to bathe – otherwise I would have taken a dip.' I assume she means it was just 'too cold' to take a dip, unless she's a masochist. Elvira Eidnes Andersen adds a little later, 'Wow!' and that is the end of that. Or at least it was until Leader Number Two added a short video of the crew running down the huge dune at the western end of the beach. We also may have – by which I mean did – manage to add a photo (I'm still not sure how) which relates to a previous Explorer trip along the Great Glen Way, but has nothing whatsoever to do with Rispond Beach. I have no idea how to remove it, and I don't think the beach does either…

Rispond beach itself

Durness is an attractive corner of the Scottish mainland with plenty going on even in October. It's certainly true to say a lot of businesses were closed up for the season, but still, there was enough going on to divert a busload of youths. I've passed through the area at the height of summer and still couldn't describe it as mobbed; only the most intrepid tourist goes so far north, with the majority staying roughly along the route of the Caledonian Canal. I'm writing this almost a year after our Scottish tour took place and since then we've been back to walk all of the Great Glen Way. At times, the length of the Great Glen looked like a Scottish-themed park – Alton Towers but with midgies, fudge and shortbread, and – not forgetting – the ubiquitous Loch Ness Monster tat. With its coach parties, hire cars and so-slow motor homes, the Great Glen is a finely honed machine designed to extract the absolute maximum amount of cash from visitors. That's not a bad thing, of course, it's their livelihood and for the most part, it is executed with subtlety and élan, and where it's not, it's entertainingly kitsch and naff. Durness wasn't like that. For a start, even when it's not windy, it feels windswept and having seen it during the high and low season, it feels desolate either way. The main attraction in Durness is probably Smoo Cave, not least for its odd name but also for its quiet grandeur, and it really is quite big. If you're lucky, the most bored geologist in the world – a wild-haired wiry man in a wetsuit – will show you around. Unfortunately, when we arrived he was securing his inflatable boats. We smiled and waved winsomely, but he was resolutely finished for the day.

Smoo Cave, Durness

I've been on the tour and can say, if you're passing, it's worth the £2 suggested cost. As you make your way down the steep path from the car park, look across the narrow cove leading to the grotto and you will see messages and names written with rocks carried from the bay below (or pinched from existing messages) on the opposite bank.

Once you get down to the footbridge over the Smoo Burn, the gaping maw of Smoo Cave reveals itself. Inside, dwarfed by the proportions of the cave itself, intrepid adventurers will see a trestle table next to a covered wooden walkway, which takes paying visitors to the inner sanctum. Amateur spelunkers (the name given to those who explore caves for a hobby), once they've deposited the proper tariff, are directed along the covered walkway to the inner cave where an inflatable boat bobs in the dark water. But what really catches the eye is the Smoo Burn as it drops 20 metres through the sinkhole in the roof. I know what you're thinking: 'But why is the Smoo Cave so interesting?' Well, I'll tell you right now – hold on to your hats people. Smoo Cave is interesting because the outer cave was formed by the sea but the inner caves and chambers came courtesy of freshwater erosion, and as the youth of today (and some geologists) like to point out – this is #totesamazeballs.

During the tour I took a while ago, a pal and I – incongruous in our bike gear – climbed down from the platform and huddled at the back of the boat, where we were joined by a Spanish couple and their young son. Our tour guide - I hope he wouldn't be offended by that title – certainly knew his stuff, providing a constant flow of information about the cave system. However, we got the impression he was a frustrated geologist stuck in a cave he had long ago become bored with. During the paddle across the inner chamber toward the waterfall (sadly not in spate during our visit) our guide scattered breadcrumbs on the water causing resident fish to feed enthusiastically. He looked at us earnestly and whispered, 'Piranha fish...' My friend and I smiled uncertainly while the young Spanish boy burst into tears. Nevertheless, we regarded the inflatable boat with new trepidation and wondered about our guide – if Ernst Stavro Blofeld emerged from behind a rock, none of us would have been surprised, I'm pretty sure he kept Piranha fish. Eventually, after ducking under a rock bridge formation, the boat scrunched up against a shale beach – the inner area of the cave was moodily lit, so we could see a small man-sized opening which our guide encouraged us to explore. It got quite warm and damp and took on a Jules Vern feel – for just a moment I felt like Doug McClure journeying to the centre of the Earth.

On this more recent visit, we settled for exploring the outer cave, which is still worthwhile – it's quite grand. After poking around and posing for photos, we emerged from the gloom blinking in the bright October sunshine for some lunch.

Durness proper, about half a mile on from Smoo Cave, is a nice wee place; you could base yourself there and enjoy a holiday. There are plenty of beaches to explore, old kirks to visit and if art and crafts is your thing, there's even more of that on offer at Balnakeil Craft Village a short walk to the west. The craft village itself (Balnakeil Village proper is a bit further on) occupies some old MOD buildings previously used to operate a cold war early warning system. The objective was to detect incoming rockets fired from Northern Russia, but it seems those pesky Russians upgraded their squibs and the new radar system became obsolete before it was officially deployed. The buildings, which to this day still show hints of a military bearing, now couldn't be more different from their original purpose, and our reason for visiting was in one of them – Cocoa Mountain. We'd all heard of this place but were only reminded of it when we saw signs for the craft village. On seeing the advertising for Cocoa Mountain, several shrieks rose up from the rear causing the minibus to veer off the main road and head for Balnakeil. The craft village was quite busy although many of the businesses seemed to have shut down for the winter. We watched two young people on mopeds enjoy a hot chocolate – they had to be local, it would take them a lifetime to get anywhere more built-up on those tiny machines. We all had a good sniff about, lots of arty galleries (not really for us I'm afraid), a hairdresser and masseuse and what turned out to be a tattoo parlour. Imagine the look on a parent's face if their child returned from camp with a tattoo – yikes. And, of course, Cocoa Mountain – the most arresting thing about it was the chocolatey smell, at least until you got inside and saw the prices. Even the cheapest thing on the notice board caused hearts to pound and a fight or flight reaction to take hold. They do a 'Dinky 9 box' for £17.50 – that's £17.50 for NINE CHOCOLATES! I don't often deploy exclamation marks (they're so melodramatic) but good grief! They must have taken a leaf out of the Green Welly Stop's business model and were relying on American chocolate connoisseurs to buy their goods. It was all we could do to stumble out the door in mute shock. The chocolate looked so good, it smelled so nice – but it was so EXPENSIVE (I feel another exclamation mark coming on). Andrew and younger Lewis - who'd been before so were acclimatised to the prices - took it in their stride and bought hot chocolates which they supped luxuriantly, we could only look on in envy. Even the off cuts (which they call 'Shards') were ruinously expensive – £15 for a 350g bag. I know it's artisan stuff and they have extra costs being as remote as they are, but their prices are sphincter clenching. I have an idea, but please bear with me – you might have an idea how my ideas go by now. Since the craft village used to be home to a nuclear missile early warning system, instead of spending billions of pounds replacing the UK's nuclear deterrent (called Trident after the popular brand of chewing gum) why not spend the money on chocolate from Cocoa Mountain? Technically, the cash would still be going toward a vaguely militaristic nuclear purpose, but instead of a uselessly expensive missile system we'll never use, we can all have a lifetime's supply of posh chocolate. Heck, if it looks like we're going to be attacked, we can just bung our aggressors a dozen 'Double Layer Whiskey Toffee Selections' and a few bags of 'Shards'. The only downside is we might become a target because the chocolate is so good, and we'd need to be careful it doesn't end up being more expensive than the original Trident replacement.

Leaving Balnakeil and Durness was something of a milestone in our journey. Although we still had three nights left on the road, had driven over 420 miles and were as far away from home as we'd ever be, we were now sort of on our way back. Durness is really nice (you should definitely go there) but it's not quite in the corner of the Scottish mainland – Cape Wrath, another 12 miles to the west, is the true most north western corner. Getting there involves a small ferry across the Kyle of Durness and a minibus trip along the single track road to the lighthouse and tea shop – there is no other public vehicle access allowed. The Cape Wrath cliffs are a Site of Special Scientific

Interest (an SSSI) but it doesn't stop the MOD blasting the crap out of the vicinity. It's always entertaining to look at the TripAdvisor ratings, especially the terrible ones, the first of which is titled: 'An unpleasant experience at your own considerable risk'. This terrified correspondent reports: 'There are NO TOILETS at the Cape or at the Ozone Café.' (Their emphasis). Were there no bushes or – dare I say – other secluded spots available at the UK's most remote and unpopulated spot? If that wasn't bad enough, he or she says of the transport: 'These minibuses are not safe on this terrain... Many of the seats were torn and held together with Gaffa Tape and some seat belt fittings looked as though they were unlikely to work reliably.' The deeply unhappy tourist goes on to say the ferry pilot asked for help from passengers on the quay to dock the boat – a hapless volunteer (described as an 'obliging lady') slipped and fell in the water. It's not a ferry in the same sense the Arran ferry is a ferry; it's a tiny boat which holds half a dozen people. The ferryman's main failing – to me anyway – seems to be a lack of appreciation of how dumb people can be and the assumption that just because a person is in the great outdoors means they know how to behave accordingly. Take the person leaving the review for example, it's a half day trip to Cape Wrath and they can't go without a bog break for the duration, or are squeamish about a quick squat behind a bush? How did they manage to get to Durness in the first place? In finishing, the helpful (but unhappy) TripAdvisor user tells us: 'All this is a terrible shame for highland tourism the sooner this attraction is in the hands of those with a real passion for the area the better, unless you really must visit Cape Wrath I wouldn't bother. If you do then take lots of care and use the toilets at Durness before you leave for the ferry.'

Respectfully, Cape Wrath is one of Scotland's last remaining genuine wilderness areas, there is nothing like it in the UK south of the central belt. It's not an attraction, it is largely untamed country – any toehold we might have on it is fleeting. It's a single track road over inhospitable land to a lighthouse which casts its light over some of the most treacherous waters in the northern hemisphere. It's not a plastic theme park with a burger franchise and easy access toilets – it's supposed to be challenging because it is challenging, you daft cotton-wool clad dope.

The point is, and it's the same with the Cocoa Mountain, Cape Wrath and everything around it is just so remote and not on the way to anywhere. You can't load up a lorry or van and say to the driver, 'Here, drop this off at Durness on your way to, ummm…' That said, Highland Council might give a little ground on the toilet situation at The Ozone Café and could help the local operators invest in a slightly bigger boat – one that at least can fill the minibus in one trip… And people who take their dogs? You might be in the most desolate spot in all of the British Isles, but other people do like to visit, so you still need to pick up after your animal. I love dogs, I'm a dog person – what I'm not is a-person-who-doesn't-pick-up-after-their-dog person. If I was in charge, I would deploy large hovering robots that would rub a dog owner's face in the dog poop if he or she neglected to clear it up. (Fortunately, I'm not in charge and sadly, there's no such thing as a hovering robot – at least not with the ability to rub lazy dog owner's faces in dog shit.)

So the top left hand corner of Scotland (as you look at it on the map) consists of a neat square set at a jaunty angle; Rispond Beach sits in the north eastern corner and Cape Wrath sits in the north west. In the south west you will find a tiny hamlet named Oldshoremore (and what looks like some lovely sandy bays) and in the south east, the bulk of Foinaven – falling short of Munro status by a mere 11ft – sits as if on guard. The road south from Durness bisects this square slightly east of centre in a fairly straight line and it is without a doubt the most remote bit of road we'd been on, easily beating the road up the western banks of Loch Eriboll. As I write this, I'm tracing our route on Google Earth; I well remember driving along that road and how it made us feel. But you get no sense of the vast emptiness, no hint of just how remote and inaccessible the land is. You can't walk too far from the road because you'll end up completely bogged down (or what we call baw-deep-in-a-bog.) The views go on for miles. Okay, more expansive views can be had elsewhere on the planet, but being in that environment was special, at least it was to me and Leaders Number Two and Three who said as much as we trundled along. I've only ever witnessed similar unadulterated views while on top of Ben Nevis or perhaps Ben Macdui, where you can almost see the curvature of the Earth. We stopped on the flanks of a mountain called Farmheall, not especially high, but still forbidding in the landscape, and tried to persuade our young charges to be quite and just listen. No traffic, no wind to speak of, no birdsong – nothing except the beep of digital cameras as selfies were taken and the chirps of mobile phones as cameras were held ready in anticipation of someone going baw-deep-in-a-bog. (Sadly, no one did.)

Desolate and remote, lonely and windswept (even though it was a still day), unpopulated, deserted and isolated – all words one could use to describe the landscape. But never barren, dreary or forsaken – I don't think any of us considered it inviting as such, but standing at the side of that road, no one was in any doubt that in our country, we'd probably never be as far away from modern civilisation as we were at that moment. We were standing in one of the most awe-inspiring yet forbidding environments Scotland has to offer. And no, there was no mobile phone signal either, which we'd got used to by that stage.

Moving out of the jaunty square and round the base of Foinaven, the scenery changed. Gone were the uniform green and brown tracts of grass, glen and mountain – we were now in the land of water and rocky hillock. The road itself becomes something of a triumph of civil engineering as it wends its way through the landscape. Past Gualin House and several attractive lochans, we made our way through Rhiconich, a tiny hamlet at the top of Loch Inchard – we were now officially on the west coast of Scotland. The word rugged may as well have been invented for the road to Laxford Bridge – which really is just a bridge. I know I keep saying this, but mere words don't do it justice – the road literally carves its way through the rocky landscape and slaloms around disgustingly picturesque lochans. We steered the minibus off the A838 and onto the A894 just after Laxford Bridge and entered yet more irritatingly beautiful scenery. It was as if the very land itself was once molten and made chaotic by unknowable forces rising from deep within the Earth's crust – only to be cooled in an instant by an omnipotent yet artful god.

Which I think is quite poetic, so not like me. I was going to say it was like the land had pulled a funny face only for the wind to change thus freezing it in place, but it didn't have the same zing. Suffice to say even our passengers were taken with the drama of the landscape.

Beyond Laxford Bridge to Scourie, it's more of the same – nature truly is a bad ass when it comes to set design. As the road unfurls, endless vistas of rock and water shot through with myriad hues of green appear. I suppose sitting in the rear of the van meant the young folk (sadly) didn't have the same views we did – truly, words did not and cannot do what we saw justice. Although we couldn't see it from the minibus, from the air, the landscape around Rhiconich, Scourie and Kylesku looks like a tray of brittle toffee shattered into a million pieces. Geologists put it rather differently. Are you ready? Here goes: most of the area from as far north as Cape Wrath and Durness down to Laxford Bridge (according to some boffins at Leeds University) is known as 'Laxfordianised Lewisian Basement'. I have no idea what that actually is, so I Googled it. If I'm being honest, that didn't really help. Get this: 'The Lewisian complex or Lewisian gneiss is a suite of Precambrian metamorphic rocks that outcrop in the north western part of Scotland, forming part of the Hebridean Terrane. These rocks are Archean and Paleoproterozoic age, ranging from 3.0 -1.7 Ga.' (From Wikipedia.) A 'Ga' means a billion years by the way – so it's really old. It's also really complicated. I was hoping to find an easier-to-digest account from someone like Dr Iain Stewart (who's television shows are soporific and fascinating in equal measure) but no, there is no *North West Scotland Geology for Dummies* that I can find. From what I can gather, it's tectonic, has something to do with the Scourie Dykes and the possible involvement of a glacier or two during one or more ice ages. I'm sorry I can't be more precise, but the more I read the more I am presented with words I understand about as well as I can pronounce, which is to say, not at all and not very well.

Scourie passes for a significant settlement in that part of the land having as it does a post office, a filling station, several B&Bs and a hotel, a campsite and three distinct streets. It even has a huge factory which supplies all of Europe with scouring pads – hence the name. Obviously, I made that up, there is no scouring pad factory. *Scourie* is another name for a young seagull, or so I read. We might have camped at Scourie but it being October meant most of the tourist infrastructure was closed for the season. Again, travelling in October might mean you avoid the midgies and many would argue (us included) the worst of the wet weather, but a lot of hotels, campsites and B&Bs close their doors on the 1st of October, so we skimmed through in our sumptuously appointed transport without stopping.

Two miles or so on from Scourie are the communities of Upper and Lower Badcall on the bay of the same name. They sound like the kind of place Dr Who might visit in his Tardis to vanquish Daleks – or I might be talking rubbish because I don't really watch Dr Who. Nevertheless, it is an interesting name for a place. Upper Badcall is the larger of the two settlements and a crofting township (when it isn't home to the Silver Nemesis, which I'm told is a baddie from Dr Who). Lower Badcall is smaller and houses the area's fishing industry consisting mostly of factory farming out in the bay, or at least that's the official story – who knows what they're really 'farming' out in the bay (cue Dr Who music). The road passes through yet more verdant scenery – fresh water lochans surrounded by rocky promontories – until eventually it descends down to sea level at Kylestrome and Kylescu with the bulk of Quinag looking on from the south. There used to be a free ferry at Kylesku but it was replaced by a bridge in 1984, a graceful concrete arc high above the water that was so handsome we stopped to take some pictures.

Somewhere between Durness and Kylesku we had 'A Moment': a short period of time which was as close to perfection as it is possible to be. A companionable silence had settled in the van, the road began to dive and soar over the landscape in a most agreeable way. As the van breached each of the road's many crests, another stunning panorama would lay itself out for us, the landscape somehow contriving to become even more attractive than it already was. We're a modern bunch so had connected Leader Number Two's phone to the van's entertainment system (he had on it music a lot more current than could be found on my phone – I'm still enthralled by midi files). An entrancing bit of electronica from Coldplay called 'Midnight' came on; it started out quietly but slowly permeated into our collective conscience. I can't adequately explain it here, but the scenery and the impromptu silence coupled with that song made for an instance we talk about even now. For the time it lasted, it was a truly beautiful moment in every regard. It's very difficult to describe and I suppose if I was able, it might not have been 'A Moment' at all. Not sure about the young people, but for the leaders, it typified that leg of our adventure. Whenever we hear that song, it reminds us of the landscape and the mood of the trip. It's one of the reasons we do it, as it's as much an experience for us as it is for the young people.

On the road with van fever developing

We'd been on the road for a while and still had a distance to go –
over fifty miles. That might not seem a lot, but on roads in the far
north west of mainland Scotland, it's a distance worth considering.
Your average speed in a minibus is going to be low, certainly no
more than 40mph and stops are frequent. We were after all on
holiday so in no particular rush, and while we could have stopped
more often than we did, we still had to pick our moments. So we
trundled on. From the Kylesku bridge, we followed the road past the
bulk of Quinag which was now firmly to the west of us. Loch Assynt
was the next landmark of note and soon enough its silvery blue
waters appeared in the distance. We joined the A837 and turned east
along the banks of the loch, past Ardvreck Castle and Inchnadamph

– a small hamlet consisting of a few houses and a hotel and lodge. Although we had no idea at the time (we didn't even stop) it turns out the caves above the settlement contain bone fragments from a variety of animals, including polar bears – the only evidence of their presence in Scotland. These old bones have been found to be as old as 47,000BP (which stands for Before Paul, I had no idea they used me as a datum point in these matters). The area is popular with geologists, although we didn't see any as we swept through the area, or at least we saw no viable candidates. The Moine Thrust runs through the landscape, which according to sources on the internet, means it's a popular place of study – its Wikipedia article goes on to say the Moine Thrust was the first of its kind to be found in the world. Suffice to say, it's all interlinked with what we talked about (somewhat inexpertly) a few pages ago. It's part of a belt of geological features running from Loch Eriboll down to the Isle of Skye – again, we'd need Dr Ian McDonald to explain. Also BP doesn't stand for Before Paul - that would be ridiculous – it stands for Before Present and by 'Present', geologists mean around 1950 when carbon dating became common. Needless to say, that technological breakthrough predates my glorious although somewhat less useful arrival by over 20 years. Mind you, what's 20 years out of 47,000 – it may as well stand for Before Paul.

From the gloriously named Inchnadamph (which, as far as I'm concerned, is certainly equal to Auchtermuchty as the go-to Scottish place name to use when practicing a broad Scots accent – you're trying it on for size right now, aren't you?) the road took us further south toward the junction at Ledmore then on to Elphin where we stopped to peruse some information boards and views I'll inadequately describe now as really nice. To the north west we could see Suilven; to the east, the twin peaks of Col Mor; and to the north, Ben Mor Assynt and Conival - both Munros over 3000ft and all very pointy and intimidating in the distance. While Leaders Number One, Two and Three admired the view, our Explorer Scouts stretched their legs and took advantage of a window of mobile phone reception to update statuses, profiles and take pictures. The crofting village of Elphin sits in the extreme south of the North West Highlands Geopark – we'd just driven down its spine from Loch Eriboll, and were now approaching one of its most eye-popping features: the Knockan Crag. I say eye-popping, it's not the Grand Canyon or anything, but it is a really long cliff, almost 10 miles long. It's a surface manifestation of the Moine Thrust, which we've mentioned before. I think we also said it was famous in geological circles, the reason for this is the Knockan Crag was formed when very old rock was forced up and over rock that was a lot younger, and for a long time, that made no sense. Along came geologists Benjamin Peach and John Horne – brace yourselves, I'm about to get geological again. Much older and heavier Moine schists (a schist is a type of rock) seemed to be sitting on top of much younger Durness Limestone, which at that time didn't really sit well with the theory of sedimentary formation, a.k.a Neptunism (so called because it was thought the Earth's endlessly powerful oceans laid down layer upon layer of ocean-carried sediment that formed the landscape geologists saw before them). Instead, Horne and Peach posited the notion that the Moine Thrust couldn't have been formed by Neptunism, but by tectonic action fuelled by Vulcanism far beneath the Earth's crust over millennia – otherwise known as Plutonism.

The view from Elphin. Our borrowed van with Canisp above and Suilven to the left

Geology is one of those topics where the more you read the more you realise you don't know. With that in mind, I think it's best if we park any further chat on the subject because if I was to continue, I'd only be waffling and moving ever further away from accuracy. I will say this though, incredibly massive things are moving beneath our feet, but they're moving so slowly, we don't notice – except when there's an earthquake, which of course we do. The pressure required to move the rocks in the Moine Thrust are massive – we're talking about billions of tons, whole cubic miles of rock being shoved up and over even more rock. In a previous short travelogue (which I feel sure you've read) we talked about 'The Doon' near Blackwaterfoot on Arran. It's a huge outcrop of rock that was once horizontal but over millennia was made to stand on its end by Vulcanism and tectonic movement. Over the years the surrounding softer rock and sediment was eroded by weather and water leaving a huge 'sill' pointing up at the sky. Interestingly (or not) Drumadoon Point on Arran has much in common with the iconic Devils Tower in Wyoming – made famous in the film *Close Encounters of the Third Kind*. It is said that Richard Dreyfus, while filming the scene where he sculpts a model of Devils Tower out of mashed potato and what might be meat loaf (to the increasing alarm of his family), based his sculpture on Drumadoon Point in Arran.

That just isn't true, I made it up.

By now we were drawing close to the junction that would take us onto the minor road to our campsite at Altandhu. It goes without saying, the scenery was still at its very best – I've run out of adequate adjectives to describe it, so I think for a while we'll talk about Scouts instead.

It might be a bit of an elephant in the room, and I think we can mostly accept that being involved with Scouts comes with certain stigmas. For example, there is always that one person who on discovering you are involved in Scouting comes to your desk and blurts out the ever hilarious 'DYB DYB DYB, DOB DOB DOB'. It is endlessly witty – truly it is. Or if in polite company, you are outed as a volunteer with a youth organisation and treated to half-joking/half-serious hints that you harbour an unhealthy interest in young boys, or that you may have a suspicious interest in uniforms and swearing-to-do-your-duty-to-God-and-the-Queen while engaging in a bit of flag idolatry.

The DYB/DOD thing stands for Do Your Best and Do Our Best, respectively. This used to be part of a mantra chanted by Cubs called the Grand Howl. I say 'used to be' because most Cub packs stopped doing it decades ago. I mean, I don't remember saying it while I was a Cub and they named a geological dating system after me. To those people who think it is a contemporary witticism? It's neither. Furthermore, if you think it is an example of playful whimsy, it's not. I'm not being over-sensitive; I won't poke your eyes out or anything, but after the thousandth time, it's about as funny as a beached whale. Moving on, there are tens of thousands of adults involved in Scouting, and they can't all be paedophiles. Well, I say that, but I make no guarantees because it does go on – suffice to say it is incredibly rare. Some time ago a conversation was overheard by leaders between some Scouts: one lad said, 'If a pedo ever tried it on with me, I'd batter him!' One of the leaders said quietly to another, 'Aye? Don't flatter yourself, son.' An older Scout he was talking to said 'Beggars can't be choosers...' It is a serious problem when it happens, but it's very rare, and we shouldn't make any more of it than is appropriate. (Also, that kid *was* ugly. I'm joking; he was really good looking… Oh dear… You see? You can't win.)

On uniforms, promises and flags, I have less of a defence except to say it is a bit outdated. Personally, I don't wear a uniform, as I just think it's a bit naff and old-fashioned, I also don't insist my Explorer Scouts wear one. The thing is, if we're out and about, it's good to be recognised as Scouts; it's a huge organisation so there's a fair chance we'll bump into other Scouts on our travels. One of the great positives about being involved is the camaraderie. The owner of Sandra's Backpackers Hostel was a Beaver Scout Leader – if he hadn't been, they might not have given us that box of couscous. If we bump into other Scouts, the ice is already mostly broken, so young people spend a lot less time being awkward around each other and more time getting to know one another.

Sometimes though, Leaders disagree, and that brings us to God, the Queen and the flag.

Firstly, God. We've done away with God – not literally, we're not devil worshippers. There is now the option of not including any mention of him, her or it, or whatever you hold him, her or it to be. We're now a movement that accepts people of all faiths and none. There are several version of the Scout promise to suit all hues of faith and of none – I'd say that was a good thing. We are after all asking people (leaders included) to make a solemn promise, which up until recently, if we had no religion, meant we all had to cross our fingers.

Secondly, the Queen. There are those who take the Queen to mean the country, the government of the day or parliament – they may not be keen monarchists but are comfortable with a slight compromise. Those of us who don't believe in the idea of the Queen and really don't want to compromise, by which I mean even acknowledge the concept of a hereditary monarchy, still have to cross our fingers or just mumble. I'd offer alternatives to that aspect of the promise too.

And finally, the flag. We are supposed to salute the Union Flag, but since I don't have a uniform, I don't salute it; therefore the flag is moot for me. Flags can be emotive to some, but I don't see the point in getting over-excited about it. I certainly wouldn't ban it: for some it's a rally point, while for others it's a butcher's apron – members should be given the choice. Most Scout groups have their own Scout flag, so perhaps there should be an option to salute that instead? To be honest, I'm not comfortable saluting anything these days – it just seems a wee bit odd to me. You might be wondering why I'm still involved, but it's the Scout Laws that count as it seems to me they constitute pretty decent advice for anyone:

1. A Scout is to be trusted.
2. A Scout is loyal.
3. A Scout is friendly and considerate.
4. A Scout belongs to the worldwide family of Scouts.

5. A Scout has courage in all difficulties.
6. A Scout makes good use of time and is careful of possessions and property.
7. A Scout has self-respect and respect for others.

There they are and a finer set of morals you couldn't hope to find, right? Especially if you replace the word 'Scout' with 'Person'. I'm not being wishy-washy here, but I really do believe that if more people – world leaders in particular – followed the Scout Law, the world would be a much nicer place.

The truth is Scouts opens up a world of opportunity for everyone who cares to get involved. Young folk get to participate in adventurous activities, have new experiences they otherwise wouldn't have and learn valuable skills – especially for the coming zombie apocalypse – and adult volunteers get to revisit their youth. What's not to enjoy about that? I'm not joking about the zombie apocalypse; I've done some research and discovered that a Scout is statistically far more likely to survive a zombie outbreak than a non-Scout, because tomahawk and knife throwing skills are Scouting activities. I'm joking about the research, it's just what I think. I'm not joking about the axe and knife throwing though. Courses are now offered at many official Scout camps. Just imagine the scene: you and your family are being chased down a lonely woodland track pursued by several of the brain-hungry undead, then all of a sudden several dull thwacks sound through the forest and the recently-risen fall back down dead with tomahawks, axes and knifes protruding from their festering skulls. The sight of a bunch of Scouts coming to retrieve their weaponry would be just as odd as the zombie outbreak was in the first place – it would be surreal, horrifying and excellent all at the same time.

We're not envisaging a zombie outbreak as such (although it's also a good skill for alien invasions – you never know) but we'll be doing axe and knife throwing skills in the near future – after all, we all know what the scout motto is, right?

As of 2014, there were around 430,000 young people involved in Scouting in the UK from age 6 to 18, led by just over 114,000 adult volunteers. Around 90,000 of those young people are girls, but for some it's still a bone of contention. We rather hoped having girls aboard would temper the wilder behaviour of the boys, but it didn't really. In fact nothing changed really, we just got wild girls in, which I suppose is as it should be. Across the world (as of 2010) there were 36 million registered Scouts and 10 million Guides, which highlights another bone of contention: Scouting in the UK became fully co-education some time ago yet Girl Guides did not reciprocate. You might think boys wouldn't want to join Guides but many leaders said (and still do say) that isn't the point; Scouts had opened its doors to all so Girl Guides should do the same. Some Scout Leaders have accused the Guide Association of sexism, although in their defence I think it was probably easier for Scouts to make the transition to a mixed model than it might be for Guides. I don't feel particularly strongly one way or the other and it's very hard to keep up with what is politically correct these days. However, if a young person (or adult) self-identifies as a female, they can now join guides, but there are still no boys allowed. Either way – we'll take anyone (whatever way you self-identify) – as long as you're prepared to swear to do your duty to a hereditary monarch, although you could chop out the word 'the' in 'the Queen' and swear allegiance to the band. The young crowd might not get that reference – you youngsters can just cross your fingers.

When the word remote is deployed to describe a place, it's not just a function of distance. Altandhu, our objective that day, was only ten miles from Ullapool as the crow flies, but it's a good bit more by road. When you factor in the condition of the road, it's further still. It was late afternoon by the time we arrived at the turn off for Achiltibuie, but there was still plenty of daylight left to pitch tents although the wind had picked up a fair bit. What can one say about the road though? If you're prone to travel sickness, you won't enjoy it. It's a single track road that swoops and swerves round hillocks, and has plenty of blind corners so you can never really maintain any speed – approximately fifteen interminable miles of lurching from left to right, up and down, back and forth, and faster and slower; sometimes individually or any combination of all four. For that reason, among others, we all still agree it was our most remote overnight spot of the trip. I would say the road meanders its way between Stac Pollaidh and Loch Lurgainn but that's far too mild an adjective; I've already used lurched so we'll go for staggered perhaps, or careened. Stac Pollaidh (often spelled Stack Polly, which if I ever had need of one, could be my drag name) isn't a particularly high mountain (2000ft), but it is very fetching to look at with its gullied, difficult-to-reach peak. Here's one for the pub quiz team: it is thought the top of Stac Pollaidh was a *nunatak* or glacial island (part of a ridge or peak system that poked above the ice sheet) and while the sides where scoured smooth as the glacier moved past, the top was left exposed to the elements to be weathered and eroded. Because it is so close to the road, it's a popular hill to climb. It is surprising to realise the feathery footfalls of so many climbers could damage something that had survived the megaton friction of a glacier, but Scottish Natural Heritage had to install a system of escalators to get climbers to the top to save its fragile flanks from further erosion. Of course, by system of escalators, I mean a path – or so I read.

Apropos of nothing other than it occurred to me when I typed the words 'pub quiz team' above, a popular question on the pub quiz circuit is: What is the nearest galaxy to Earth? The answer they'll look for will invariably be the Andromeda Galaxy in the constellation of the same name, also known as M31 or NGC224. It's 2.5 million light-years away but still visible with the naked eye, but it's far from being the closest. Up until 1994 the Large Megellanic Cloud (or LMC) was (and still is) a good deal closer at 160,000 light-years. However, the closest galaxy to us is a dwarf elliptical galaxy in Sagittarius, imaginatively named the Sagittarius Dwarf Elliptical Galaxy – which is only 70,000 light-years away. The quiz master won't thank you for pointing any of that out by the way – you will be branded a pedant and troublemaker (or in my case, he'll just look at you as if you're from a Dwarf Elliptical Galaxy in Sagittarius). It's probably best just to say the Andromeda Galaxy or maybe M31 if you want to score a minor point, even if only in your own head. (If you want to be a proper smart arse, if the question 'what is the nearest star to planet Earth?' pops up, you might say the sun. This, while correct, is a high risk strategy, as the answer they're looking for may well be Alpha Centauri. If it is, you could mildly point out that Alpha Centauri is actually three stars locked together by gravity – the quiz master might then look at you as if you're from there too…)

As I typed all that out, it occurred to me, readers might think I couldn't possibly know so much about the cosmos, so must be some kind of insufferable smart arse. This isn't *exactly* the case, for years, from age 12 to 28 or so, I went to an astronomy club. That might sound nerdy and sad, but we mostly ate biscuits and laterally, went to the pub, having said that, a lot of the astronomy stuck. As I keep saying to my Explorers and Scouts (and anyone else unfortunate enough to be within earshot), astronomy is a subject about which you only need to know a little, to appear a lot cleverer than you really are.

It could also be that it makes you come across as a bumptious twat, which would explain why Explorers and Scouts so far haven't shown any interest in my astronomy lectures…

Anyway, I digress. The road dived and cork-screwed its way to Achnahaird Bay on the north coast of the peninsula then turned south and back on itself round a myriad of tiny lochans to the southern coast and Altandhu with its views toward the Summer Isles.

Again, there are various adjectives I could deploy, but none of them will do the place justice. What I will say is this: I want to go back, I've wanted to go back ever since I left – we all do. When we booked in that morning in Thurso, which seemed so long ago and so far away, we had no idea how remote it would feel or how peaceful – even with the howling wind. The campsite looked brand new. If you look for it on Google Earth you won't find it, as the images aren't up-to-date enough to show it. The Am Fuaran bar is there, but that's all. Lewis and I stumbled into the bar on wobbly minibus legs to find the owner was away to Ullapool on errands, so instead we went back out to look for a suitable place to pitch our tents. The site wasn't busy; there were maybe half a dozen intrepid motor homes and one small van with a makeshift awning, and in the centre a generously proportioned, brand spanking new toilet, kitchen and shower block. We ended up plumping for a bit of flat grass at the top of the site somewhat sheltered behind a small bungalow. Normally we like to be away on our own so we don't bother anyone, but the wind was gusting quite strongly and our tents were in danger of being blown flat.

We sat for a while in the van as it was rocked gently by the wind. Our Explorers were away – well, exploring, I suppose - but soon returned because there's not much to see. Altandhu consists of the bar, the smokehouse (which was closed), the campsite and maybe a dozen houses within eyesight. You might wonder why we're still so keen to return. It was a mixture of things, even with the strong winds and the absence of someone who could tell us if we were okay to pitch our tents in the lee of the bungalow. I'll try to explain: Achiltibuie is the main village in a string consisting of Altandhu, Polbain, (Achiltibuie), Polglass, Badenscallie and Achvraie, situated in that order from west to east with views over the Summer Isles. The location is remote – properly remote and beautiful in its ruggedness – and untouched by modernity. It's described on Undiscovered Scotland as '...*the north west of Scotland as it used to be twenty or thirty years ago...*' and '...*not for those who like their Scotland neatly packaged in shops selling tartan dolls waving Saltires.*' It's also not on the way to anywhere, you need to be coming here to get here, you'll never pass through by accident and think, 'Ooooh, this is nice" – it takes a real effort, even on four wheels. As if to underline the nature of the place, as we sat peacefully watching our young people amble back up the hill to the van, a gate opened at the far corner of the campsite and hundreds of sheep spilled through guided by two sheep dogs and a shepherd we could hear whistling but couldn't quite see. The sheep moved as a group but soon split up around campervans and other obstacles only to be guided back into manageable clumps by the dogs at the command of the still invisible shepherd. Every now and again they would stop to chomp hungrily at the grass until one of the dogs moved them on. Eventually the mostly reformed herd found its path blocked by our Explorers. They split again into several different groups and found fresh grass to chew on (the sheep, not our Explorers). Eventually, after much whistling (from the now visible shepherd), dog manoeuvring and a man on a quad bike, the sheep left the campsite, crossed the road into a different field next to the pub and all was peaceful again.

Eventually the site owner returned and gave us the go ahead to pitch our tents (and cook under the shelter of the kitchen block). We dragged Andrew away from the tussock of grass he was hungrily chewing and got our camp organised for the night ahead.

A quick word from TripAdvisor about the site, there aren't many reviews but they're all good, except one, which is 'terrible'. As I read it, my heart dropped because the complainant may have been talking about us. Fortunately, reading on, the details in the review began to diverge from the reality of our visit. I also checked the date of the review – turns out it was submitted months before we were there. It's possible we're being too forgiving but in the off season in a place that isn't on the way to anywhere (so no passing trade) and with the owners having other things to do – as I see it, even in the high season – they can't be there all the time. As the writer from Undiscovered Scotland points out – this is the north west of Scotland as it was twenty or thirty years ago. That you might have to wait for something, even for an hour is just something you need to get used to. The reason I thought 'Jane O from Liverpool' might have been talking about us was because we cooked our tea that night in the lea of the amenity block and we also used the handy tables and chairs provided to sit down and eat. We also hung around for a while inside the building (which did have a small seating area) because it was so windy – we thought since we were paying for the facilities, we may as well use them. These were all things 'Jane O' was bumping her gums about – that and the notion there was no one around with whom she could register a complaint. But it wasn't us who ruined her Achiltibuie experience – no irritable Liverpudlian came over to tell us to be quiet at 1am because we were in bed, and anyway, at that point it wasn't possible to hear anything except the wind.

The Am Fuaran bar was nice though. We decided to leave our Explorers to tidy up the dinner detritus and do what ever it is teenagers do of an evening in the middle of nowhere while we went for a civilised drink. There are those who'd say this was selfish, and to those people I'd say, you may well be right. I suppose we could have sat down in the communal area of the amenity block with the young people, but do you know what? All week we'd tried to understand and involve ourselves in the chat – and pretty much couldn't. We needed some adult time, so we were going to the pub. We opened the door and froze, the floor had obviously just been mopped and we didn't want to clomp all over it with our muddy boots. Lewis looked a wee bit closer and said, 'Eh, no, it's not wet, it's just really shiny.'

I said, 'Away man, it's soaking, look at it...' or words to that effect. I had to reach down and touch the black stone-tiled floor to be sure, and sure enough it was as dry as a bone, but just very heavily lacquered. I'm not saying this is a reason to drive all that distance to the back of beyond then drive a good bit further, but it was truly, the shiniest floor I have ever seen.

There was also a pool table and a bar with lager on tap – it would have been rude not to. Lewis, Michael and I played a few games of pool and had one or two drinks until the young folk found us and shamed us into returning to the campsite. They'd spent the night playing cards in the amenity block, and I should say again, it wasn't just toilets, showers and a kitchen, it had a small open area which contained the tables and chairs we'd used at dinner time – they weren't actually playing cards in the bogs. At one point they all disappeared – as in completely disappeared. Which brings us to the next reason for wanting to return; it was so dark with absolutely no light pollution what-so-ever. The night sky was mostly clear above and there was no Moon, and although there were some lights round the campsite, several of our Explorers had lain down in shadows cast by grassy mounds on the site and all but disappeared into the inky darkness. Urban living means we tend not to see the night sky at its best, but here the stars, despite the odd cloud here and there, were startlingly clear and sharp. So clear in fact that it was difficult to unravel the constellations you can usually see from the background clutter of stars you normally can't. It is a really special place.

There wasn't much else to do except go to bed earlier than we otherwise might. The wind hadn't abated but our tents were holding their own for the moment – being in them could only improve their chances of not being blown away.

The Port a Bhaigh campsite by Altandhu

People like to talk about the romanticism of camping: the light patter of raindrops on canvas, the gentle susurration of the night's breeze as it whispers around the guy lines, but I'm not so sure though. It's very hard to wax lyrical about sleeping in a hike tent. The following morning I found out Lewis and Michael had similar experiences to me: they'd also been kept awake by the violent snapping of nylon as the wind blasted its way between the flysheet and inner tent.

Fortunately, it didn't rain, but if it had I think we would've ended sleeping in the bogs down the hill… Boy was it windy, though; there was just no let up. I lay in a state of semi-consciousness, and every few seconds a particularly enthusiastic blast of wind would roll down the hills from behind the Am Fuaran bar and cause the material of my tent to flap against my face. I don't know if wind boarding is a thing, and I don't imagine it would compare to water boarding, but it was certainly annoying. At some point in the early hours I heard the telltale snap of a fibreglass tent pole (professional Scout Leaders can tell this noise at many paces). There isn't much that is good about having to get up in the middle of the night while on Scout camp: a tent has either fallen down, someone is homesick, or has puked up that day's intake of Haribo and energy drink. I thought I'd better go out and have a look around, and sure enough one of our tents was in distress. The vestibule/storage area had been blown flat, but fortunately the sleeping section was still intact and snoring could be heard. I dug out the Gaffa Tape and made temporary repairs and vowed to be indoors the following night.

I know I haven't described a perfect night's camping, but it was more the feel of the place, its remote aspect and many other things I can't quite put my finger on that just made it a nice place to be. In the summer, the air would be alive with midgies and the usual gripes around campsites having some cover or indoor space (that won't annoy Jane O from Liverpool) and the odd picnic table to sit round and prepare meals still remain. Perhaps it was the pace of life – by which I mean the near total lack of it. If you have no expectation of instantaneous attention then you won't be disappointed when you don't get it. To truly appreciate it, it's not enough to travel the hundreds of miles to a spot just north of Ullapool then another fifteen miles beyond that, you need to travel back in time too. Perhaps we enjoyed it as much as we did because we had nothing to do, nothing to monitor or keep up with – no status updates or emails, tweets or phone calls to check or make – so all we could do was nothing which is pretty much what we did. I think that is unusual these days. For some it induces panic whilst for others it motivates them to say silly things on internet review sites when they get home, whilst for others, it sets them free.

I think we fell into that last category and I think the campsite owner and her young son – both of whom were born and bred in the area – seemed like good evidence for it. During our stay, we had to draw their attention to a catastrophically blocked toilet – the severity of which had witnesses wondering at the nature of the arse from which so much poo could emerge – but even so, they dealt with it with stoic aplomb.

Achiltibuie is Scottish Gaelic which means 'field of the yellow-haired boy' – isn't that nice? It's also very difficult to pronounce. It sort of goes like Achil-tae-boo-ay with prevalence on the 'tae' in the middle, which was how Ally – who would be returning to the area with his parents – told me to pronounce it.

Day six – Achiltibuie and Altandhu to Broadford

The evening view from our Altandhu campsite

Because of the wind, we had a cold breakfast on the go while we struck camp. More than once we almost lost a flysheet to the elements – it's just as well those young people still had their wits about them. Having said that, it wasn't a great idea to leave anything lighter than, say, a fully packed rucksack unattended lest it take flight. Indeed, some of our lighter members elected to keep their rucksack on just in case they themselves blew away. The last thing we did was square up with the landlady. A very reasonable fee we thought given the site's situation and amenities. The road out was the same as the road in, just the other way round. The scenery was still as nice and on the northern side of the peninsular curiously unwindy – if that's even a word. Soon we passed again under the magisterial bulk of Stac Pollaidh, but this time on the other side of the van so passengers on the left could have a look. Shortly thereafter we regained the main road to Ullapool.

Passing through Strathkanaird then Ardmair with its campsite (which looked well appointed but firmly closed at that time of year) eventually we arrived back in what passes for busy in the far north west of Scotland – the town of Ullapool.

Ullapool has much in common with Wick; it's a Thomas Telford designed town built for the herring boom in the 1780s. It's not quite as large mind, with a population of around 1500 versus Wick's 7500, but be that as it may, Ullapool does seem nicer – even if it doesn't boast any record-breaking short streets. After having spent time in some of Scotland's most remote territory, Ullapool's early morning rush hour (well fifteen minutes, say) was a bit of a shock. Having to wait in traffic (just our van and another car really) before parking up at the town's hypermarket (well, supermarket) was a bit unnerving. Looking in the rear view mirror, I could see in the eyes of my young Explorers a sudden need for sugar-laden treats like Strawberry Laces, Fizzy Haribo and cans of Red Bull just so they could keep up with the increased pace of life. Mobile phones began to chirp insistently for attention as they were engulfed in an electronic tsunami of updates from Ullapool's crowded ether. We even heard some ambitious metropolitan fireball honking his horn impatiently in the distance. Okay, it's possible as I relive our return to the urban hubbub of the town (village really) that I may have become somewhat giddy, but it was jarring.

I've been to Ullapool twice before and stayed the night in the town. First of all in the Arch Inn (very nice it was too), then the following year at the venerable old Caledonian Hotel (which served watery powdered scrambled eggs). Don't labour under the misapprehension that the Arch Inn wasn't without fault too – we asked for some tomato ketchup with breakfast and some eight years later, we're still waiting. I liked both places though; the Caledonian Hotel was one of those old-fashioned hotels so developed over the years that if there was a fire, you'd get lost in the corridors and probably die of smoke inhalation. I realise that isn't a cheery thought, far less a glowing recommendation, but how often do hotels catch fire and with all those watery scrambled eggs available, would it be allowed to get out of hand? I don't remember much about the Caledonian except that it had an all-you-can-eat breakfast buffet bar which to my mind is possibly the Best Thing Ever after world peace and Creamola Foam, and that on the way to our room, we had to step over the bodies of several OAPs who'd presumably got lost in the hotel's labyrinthine corridors and died of hunger, a lack of water or perhaps natural causes. Those coach parties should really be more diligent with their headcounts. The Arch Inn, which if I'm being honest, is the place I'd return to – lack of tomato ketchup not-with-standing. It is situated right on Loch Broom and has tables over the road at which a weary traveller can rest and sip delicately on a pint of lager while enjoying the views up and down the loch and south toward An Teallach.

Other things one should say about Ullapool in any respectable travelogue (so I genuinely have no idea why I'm bothering here) is that the ferry to Stornaway (on the Isle of Lewis) has its mainland port in the town. Also the people of Ullapool do enjoy a festival: Loopallu in September with an often impressive line up, Ullapool Guitar Festival in October, a dance festival in March and Ullapool Book Festival in May. There's also the An Talla Solais or the Talla Light Art Centre, a hub for local artists and the visual arts, and the Macphail Centre, a place for performing arts and theatre. I can't find any record-breaking facts about Ullapool, except some difficult-to-confirm hints about record-breaking trees in the area, but I could make something up though... Did you know, Ullapool holds the world record for having the most festivals per head of population? In fact, the town hosts many festivals that purport to take place in completely different places like La Tomatina, Mardi Gras or the Running of the Bulls at Pamplona - it's a little known fact, but they've all since been outsourced to Ullapool. Not a lot of people know that, mostly because it's not true.

Ullapool is a welcome blip of urbanity in the midst of a lot of beautiful nothingness, so we took the opportunity to restock our dwindling supplies (we still had the box of Couscous so wouldn't have starved) and refuel the minibus. We hadn't had a proper breakfast but we were still well short of midmorning, and besides, our young adventurers had also filled their cheeks (so to speak) with sherbet-filled Flying Saucers (the horrible rice paper ones), Mars Bars, gallons of Irn Bru and milk chocolate Jazzles from Tescos. Explorer Scouts are at that transitional age between childhood and adulthood. You can see it in their parents' eyes as they wave them away on trips like this – they're sending away their wee boy or girl and worry that an intimidating shaggy man or overly curvaceous woman will return. On balance though, I'd say it's still quite nice having to point out to a burly 15-year-old boy they have chocolate smeared up the side of their face. I'd also say, our lone female member was also lacking in the vanity stakes that assail many young women these days. I'm happy to report that Rhianna doesn't put make up on with a spatula like some young ladies seem to and prefers to be practically clothed at all times, and she also managed to eat confectionary in a most lady-like manner – I like to think she takes after me.

But I digress.

Our next stop was the Corrieshalloch Gorge, situated to the south of Ullapool on the road to the Torridons. Weary travellers can continue on the A835 which crosses back to the east coast emerging approximately at Dingwall about 50 miles away. We, on the other hand, turned left onto the A832 which skirts the west coast past Gruinard Island, Laide, Aultbea, Poolewe, Gairloch, Shieldaig (#1), Slattadale, Talladale and Kinlochewe. From there we'd cut through the Torridon mountains to the village of the same name, then on to

Shieldaig (#2), slicing through the base of the Applecross peninsula then turning east to Lochcarron and almost back on ourselves to Strathcarron. We'd then be within spitting distance of our destination for the day (our longest in terms of miles travelled) on Skye via Stromeferry (No Ferry), Auchtertyre, Balmacara and Kyle of Lochalsh. There, we'd skip over the Skye Bridge to Broadford on the Isle of Skye itself and our billet for the night – The Broadford Backpackers Hostel, so named because that is where and what it was, but we'll get to that, all in good time.

The Corrieshalloch Gorge is nice; it's a deep gash in the ground with a cheerful burn at the bottom and the Falls of Measach at its western end. The cheerful burn I mentioned is the River Droma, and its level was low when we visited, but when in spate however, the falls provide quite a sight as they plunge 45 metres into the gorge. There is the obligatory Victorian suspension bridge with which to scare yourself. (These can be found dotted round the country. There's one in the village of Tain which has a sign saying, 'DANGER – ONLY TWO PEOPLE ALLOWED ON THIS BRIDGE AT ANY ONE TIME', although it doesn't stipulate how fat the people can be.) A particular attraction at Corrieshalloch is to wait for unsuspecting tourists to cross then stride enthusiastically across with them; the entire thing develops a most disconcerting reverberation if you tread too heavily.

Of course, I'm sure it's safe. I read on the National Trust's website – they maintain the area as a nature reserve – that the bridge was designed by a fellow called Sir John Fowler, who was also one of the principle designers of the Forth Bridge. Having said that, present day engineers had to make significant renovations in 2012 after cracks and weak points were found in the foundations and cables of the bridge at Corrieshalloch – so, it's now as good as new, isn't it?

There is a modern viewing platform from which to take selfies and while it can't really compete with the Grand Canyon's Skywalk, let's do a comparison anyway. The Grand Canyon Skywalk will set you back $41 for an adult and $35 for a child, whereas the Corrieshalloch Skywalk (I'm probably not allowed to call it that) is free. On the other hand, at Corrieshalloch, there is no option to upgrade, which at the Grand Canyon would include a meal of your choice, a photo opportunity with the Hualapai people and a hop-on/hop-off shuttle bus service to all view points. I suppose the Ullapool tourist board could scare up a couple of locals if visitors really wanted a photo opportunity with the indigents and a burger van could probably be parked somewhere. I should say, it's a quid to park at Corrieshalloch so strictly speaking not entirely free; however, it is run on an 'honesty box' basis so you could just do a runner – it goes without saying, we paid.

The Corrieshalloch Gorge is 0.9 miles or 1.5km long; the Grand Canyon is 277 miles or 446km long. In terms of depth, Corrieshalloch is 200ft or 60m at its deepest point, whereas the Grand Canyon rather trumps that at 6100ft or 1857m. Width-wise it's not great news for Corrieshalloch either: the Grand Canyon is 18 miles or 30km at its widest point, the Corrieshalloch Gorge only manages 33ft or 10m. I wasn't going to make those comparisons, but I'd written down all the imperial and metric dimensions and it seemed such a shame to waste the effort I'd made to Google it. I also used a whole post-it note to jot down the figures. In closing, the Grand Canyon is so-called because it is indeed quite grand, while the Corrieshalloch Gorge is so named from the Scots Gaelic *Coire Shalach*, which means dirty or unattractive kettle, which in the context of Scots Gaelic refers to a cauldron or whirlpool. (I assume it's a description of the waterfall's plunge pool, although it looked spotless when we were there.)

Whichever it is, you should go and have a look because it's quite nice.

Back in the minibus with a slightly different combination of warning lights arranged on the dashboard for our perusal and the Couscous from Sandra's confirmed as being safely stowed, we turned right out of the car park toward Gruinard Island. I hoped our passengers weren't becoming overly bored with the travelling. Minibus seats aren't the most comfortable and while from the front we had good views, the same couldn't be said from the back. We'd also covered a lot of ground the previous day through some of the best scenery Scotland had to offer, but I wondered if perhaps a lot of the vistas to come would be lost due to boredom or insouciance. The thing is, I might be satisfied with an information board in a lay-by and the beauty of the surrounding environment, but I have enough self-awareness to know that, in the eyes of persons younger than myself, it might make me look like a boring old fart. I have since asked if they enjoyed the trip and they all said they did, although it's possible they were just being polite because they're like that.

We were now entering an area of Wester Ross (of Ross and Cromarty) known to some as The Great Wilderness, which has a satisfying tone about it. The area is dominated by An Teallach – views of which we enjoyed whilst dropping down into Ullapool that morning. It's a Munro (two in fact) with one of the more pointy ridges in between, which is always satisfying to see as some Munros are a bit dull, having a distinctly pudding-bowl shape about them, An Teallach on the other hand looked positively scary as we passed its northern slopes. You might ask why we weren't climbing any of these mountains; unfortunately, the truth is we can't. For a start, I wouldn't make it. Recently while visiting the island of Arran with Leaders Number One and Two and a couple of ex-Explorers home from university, we decided to visit the Coire Fhionn Lochan which is described on walkhighlands.co.uk as a 'straightforward moorland walk to a beautiful mountain lochan with a white gravel beach' – all of which is true except for the first three words, well, for me anyway. It's interesting and alarming how quickly one can let things go. I used to bound up Munro's ten or fifteen years ago, now though, I can't even manage a 'straightforward moorland walk'. If you ever visit Arran (and you're fitter than I am) you should do the Coire Fhionn Lochan walk – it really is beautiful. It's only 5 km or 3 miles in distance (give or take) but the ascent is 326 metres, which for me presented a serious, and at times seemingly terminal, problem. The phrase 'to die on one's arse' couldn't have been more pertinent. I remember some time ago – okay a long time ago – running up Meikle Says Law, the highest of East Lothian's Lammermuir hills. It was a 10 km or 6-and-a-bit mile run that ascended 263m to a height of 535 m, not very high by Highland standards but still I ran up it. Sometimes I ask myself what went wrong – the pork pie I'm usually holding provides a definite clue.

Fortunately, I have a good cover story for not being able to climb mountains like An Teallach with Explorer Scouts – I'm not allowed to anymore. Back in Venture Scout days (the section that existed before Explorers and Network came into being) we used to make regular trips up north to bag Munros. By the time Venture Scouts stopped, we'd climbed over forty including Ben Nevis (we did that twice), Ben Macdui (the second highest of all Scottish mountains), the Buachaille Etive Mor (three Munros including Stob Dearg, the mountain that greets you as you approach the eastern end of Glen Coe from Rannoch Moor). We completed the Ring of Steall in the Mamore Mountains above Kinlochleven – four Munros forming a loop route (the start of which we would explore on the second last day of our trip). Now though, we can't. Some might say it's health and safety gone wrong, but actually, it's for the best. I have a fair bit of experience, but taking a group of novice walkers into a dangerous environment is not something you want to do if you're not 100%

confident in your abilities – and physical ability is still somewhat important.

As in life in general, it's the bad experiences that tend to be the most instructive. I was part of a mixed group (some Venture Scouts and some highly experienced adults) who decided to take on the Aonach Eagach – this is the ridge you can see if you look north as you pass through Glen Coe. It is an iconic ridge walk involving lots of scrambling over rocky pinnacles often with no discernible safe route – when out and about in the hills, the road less travelled may be less travelled for a reason. We had a couple of novice walkers in the group who struggled with what hill walking publications innocently call 'exposure'. It's not exposure in the sense of the physical malady one might develop if out in bad weather; it's a route or path that exposes those traversing it to death if they deviate from it, even slightly. We were well prepared. We had safety ropes and while we never had to rope anyone up, we did have to take our packs off and lower them down the odd drop off so we could climb down safely. At one or two points we also found ourselves astride rocks with our legs dangling out into space. Our novice walkers weren't comfortable and if I'm being honest, I wasn't either. In hindsight, the risk involved – while nowhere near the realms of sheer idiocy – meant it was a nervous day out. Would I do it again? Well, no, because I'd die on my arse long before I got anywhere near the ridge walk itself, possibly on the outskirts of the car park.

We'd booked ourselves into the Glen Nevis Youth Hostel for that trip. After a day's walk which had been as arduous as it was nerve racking, I remember arriving to book in and there propping up the reception desk was one of those awful outdoor gigolo type people, wearing a Puffa gilet type body warmer and trousers with many zips. Standing there nonchalantly, pretending not to do so for the sole purpose of belittling other people's efforts in the great outdoors, he asked a number of questions: where, why and how long being the main ones. We told him Aonach Eagach, to walk along it and about eight hours. He wasn't impressed, but on the plus side it gave him something to feel superior about. He reported he'd done it several times and it only ever took him four hours, 'certainly no more' he told us. I'm not proud of it, but we beat the crap out of him. Okay, we never did that, but the bigger the group the longer it takes to cover your route. A group of ten people stopping at different times to pee, dig out Mars Bars and adjust straps versus one person doing it – regardless of how many zipped pockets they have to search for that Mars Bar – it just takes more time.

The point is, the ridge walk on An Teallach is also very exposed and even if I was in peak physical condition, I still wouldn't take a group up to traverse it because it would be far too risky. That's my story, and I am sticking to it

Because of our early and quite windy start, it was only midmorning as we left Corrieshalloch. I knew Gruinard Bay was the next most notable place and I'd decided, since I happened by chance to know a wee bit about the place, to take the time to be educational for a few minutes. First though – sinister stories to one side – Gruinard Bay with its island is very nice to look at; you reach it after travelling up the southern banks of Little Loch Broom then moving inland to the bay itself at a place called Mungasdale. As you travel round the bay, if you look back over your right shoulder – imagine you were in the minibus with us – you would be able to see, beyond Gruinard Island, the Summer Isles and I feel sure with good eyesight, our new favourite campsite back at Altandhu. But it's Gruinard Island itself that is interesting. It has a very chequered past, indeed much of which has been embellished and capitalised upon in popular fiction not least by authors Desmond Bagley, Frederick Forsyth and Greg Bear. I stopped the minibus in a lay-by overlooking the island and told the young people to prepare to be informed.

In the 1880s, the island's population was recorded as being six, but come the beginning of the 20th century it fell to zero. During the Second World War, it became obvious Germany was testing chemical weapons and in order to keep up so must Britain. In a joint venture between Britain, Canada and the USA, Gruinard Island was purchased for £500 from its owners and designated out of bounds to the locals for chemical warfare testing – although as you might imagine, they kept that last part quiet. Britain has form in this area – did you know, the UK Government tested atomic weapons at Montebello Islands and at Maralinga in Australia? The Maralinga test site was 800 km (about 500 miles) north west of Adelaide on the mainland. Seven – repeat SEVEN - nuclear devices were tested at Maralinga along with a number of smaller tests that led to severe contamination. The aboriginal people who lived there believed the land to be of great spiritual significance, but as you might imagine, that claim fell on deaf ears. Eventually it was stopped after Australians became incredibly angry about such a massive imposition.

But I digress.

The biological warfare testing at Gruinard was code named Operation Vegetarian, the reasons for which will become apparent. They wanted to discover if a strain of anthrax bacterium could be weaponised and used against German cows – bear with me. This involved finding out if the bacteria would survive in explosions of differing intensities, how effectively it might spread and how long it would remain. The flavour of anthrax chosen was called 'Vollum 14578', so called because an RL Vollum, Professor of Bacteriology at the University of Oxford supplied it – it's a legacy of sorts, I suppose. The tests were carried out on sheep which they purchased from local farmers then secured to specific spots on the island. Bombs clad with anthrax spores were then exploded at the top of poles (aerial bombardment was far too dangerous) and the spread of the bacillus was recorded by the trail of dead sheep. At first they seemed to have survived but after three days, they began to die in earnest and horribly. They decided after a number of tests that dropping anthrax bombs was a stupid idea; they would be completely indiscriminate, killing Allied as well as German soldiers (civilians aren't really mentioned on the Wikipedia or Secret Scotland websites). I conveyed all that to a rapt audience of Explorer Scouts. Actually, that is a lie, it looked like they'd been infected by a particularly virulent strain of the Boredom Bacterium – perhaps they can name it after me. Apparently, or so I read, Operation Vegetarian's other aim was to examine the efficacy of dropping 'cattle cakes' – linseed cakes infected with anthrax spores. It says on the Wiki page: *'These cakes would have been eaten by the cattle, which would then be consumed by the civilian population, causing the deaths of millions of German citizens. Furthermore, it would have wiped out the majority of Germany's cattle, creating a massive food shortage for the rest of the population that remained uninfected.'* How horrible is that? If you didn't get anthrax and die, then the food shortages (and presumably enforced vegetarianism) would get you a wee bit down the line…isn't war hell?

Anyway, going back to my comatose audience on the road by Gruinard Bay. In 1945, with nothing ever coming of the tests carried out, the owners applied to buy the island back as agreed. The Ministry of Supply recognised that this could not happen since the ground was still infested with deadly Vollum 14578, so they took responsibility for the island and agreed the owners could buy it back for the agreed £500 when it became safe to do so. For a long time, nothing was done. Various reasons were given, the main one being that it would be far too costly to decontaminate the island, but in reality, it was thought no one really knew how to go about it.

It doesn't stop there though. In 1981 *Operation Dark Harvest* began and this is where the fun begins. Dark Harvest was a 'campaign' waged by the Dark Harvest Commando of the Scottish Citizen's Army – a name which trips of the tongue and isn't in the least bit over the top. They wanted the island decontaminated and made safe and were prepared to engage in affirmative action to attain their objective. At some point (allegedly) two unnamed university microbiologists went onto the island with help from locals and removed as much as 140kg of contaminated earth. The group then threatened to deposit various-sized piles of it *'at appropriate points that will ensure the rapid loss of indifference of the government and the equally rapid education of the general public'*. And this they did. A package was left outside Porton Down (the UK's go-to place for all things biologically apocalyptic but more prosaically known as a United Kingdom Government Military Science Park), where it was analysed and found to contain anthrax spores. As scientists and various MOD lackeys were running around most probably shitting themselves, another package of soil was left in Blackpool, where the then Conservative government were having their conference – that one contained only muck, which at least was politically apt.

Finally, decontamination started in the late 80s, with the island being infused with tones of formaldehyde mixed with sea water and the top soil scraped off and taken away in sealed containers and presumably fired into space or something. A flock of volunteer sheep was placed on the island – don't be so cynical, they all put their hoofs up for the job – where they were monitored and found to be perfectly healthy. In 1990, a junior defence minister called Lucky McFortunate – I'm joking, his name was Michael Neubert – set foot on the island, removed the signs forbidding people access to the island and declared it safe.

There have been no cases of anthrax among the island's flock of volunteer sheep, but equally, I don't think anyone is eating them either.

A final word on Gruinard Island. After the tests during World War Two, scientists had to dispose of the sheep killed by Professor Vollum's namesake. There are two versions of this story. Version one: the carcasses were put into a cave at the base of a handy sea cliff on the island, the entrance to which was sealed with explosives. This version related in a 2001 *Telegraph* article went on to report that 'a mare, a lovely red heifer and many, many sheep', all expired, according to a local lady referred to as Mrs McIver. Apparently a storm dislodged some of the dead sheep from the rubble and the tide brought them to the mainland. The second version – from secretscotland.org.uk – is much more fun or perhaps not, dependant on your point of view. After the tests finished, animal carcasses were reported washing up on mainland beaches. Initially, this was blamed on a Greek freighter tossing dead sheep overboard. The British Government on behalf of the Greek Government even offered compensation to farmers who had animals that died from infection. In reality – or so Secret Scotland claims (and I am inclined to believe them) – the dead sheep had been placed at the base of a cliff about which explosives had been planted, with the aim of bringing said cliff down on top, thus burying the dead sheep. Unfortunately, the force of the blast propelled some of the carcasses out to sea where they were soon lost. Because reports of animals dying on the mainland were now circulating freely, the security service invented the story about Greek sailors chucking sheep over board to avoid a panic.

I think you'll agree, the second story is far more British Establishment than the first.

Travelling away from the picturesque Gruinard Bay takes you to Loch Ewe and Aultbea, both of which have a rich history in terms of military activity – British militarism is a bit of a theme in this part of Scotland. In an attempt to befuddle German intelligence during the Second World War, Loch Ewe was used as a staging post for Arctic convoys after the disaster that befell Arctic convoy PQ17. Out of 34 ships that sailed from Hvalfjord in Iceland, only eleven reached Murmansk. At first the Russians, who were desperate for supplies, thought the allies were lying about what they'd sent – they couldn't believe so many ships from one convoy could be lost. A mix of poor communication, bad intelligence on the allied side and breakthroughs in signals intelligence by the Germans led to some poor decision-making – which is something of an understatement.

From 1941, convoys gathered at Loch Ewe so they could take advantage of the greater cover and shelter. In truth, no words can do justice to the bravery of the men and boys (some of whom couldn't have been much older than those in the minibus) who travelled on these convoys. It wasn't enough that they had to contend with deathly poor weather because even at the best of times the boats in which they sailed were little more than sitting ducks for German U-Boats and Luftwaffe air raids.

Now it is home to two of the UK nuclear submarine fleet's Z-Berths – what is a Z-Berth I hear you mutter? A Z-Berth is a berth (obviously) at which Britain's fleet of 'immensely useful' nuclear submarines can resupply while its occupants can get a little R&R. There is also a NATO Petroleum, Oil and Lubricant Depot (or POL depot) at Aultbea. What doesn't happen at a Z-Berth is any maintenance of the nuclear bits of warships – that can only take place at X-Berths, or so we are told. According to Secret Scotland, there are currently five active Z-Berth locations in Scotland: Loch Ewe (four berths in all including two at the POL depot), Coulport, Loch Goil and Rothesay. There are two nuclear maintenance-enabled X-Berth locations in Scotland: at Faslane (HMNB Clyde – 8 berths in all) and at Rosyth (11 berths in total). Other X-Berths are located at Devonport (16 berths) and Barrow-in-Furness (unknown – might be top secret). In any case, as you trundle round the banks of Loch Ewe, you can see a business-like jetty out in the water, and if you look inland you can just make out the earth-covered tanks of the POL depot.

Reading about NATO X- and Z-Berths is interesting for two reasons. Firstly, the contingency planning the Navy put in place for the local population in case of a nuclear incident – locals are given a supply of potassium iodate tablets (or PITs for those in the know) and told to stay indoors. Interestingly, at Devonport they have the 'Devonport Off-Site Emergency Plan (Version 4) *Public Version*' – people might wonder what the non-public version has to say on the topic, I bet it's a lot starker. And secondly, if you say the word 'berth' too often, it begins to sound ridiculous.

Loch Ewe also contains a nice looking island of the same name – the Isle of Ewe. That it is inhabited and was busy hosting arctic convoys during World War Two ruled it out for the chemical testing that went on at Gruinard. Today, it is popular with courting couples who like to take boat trips round the island – or so I read. Apparently, its name sounds like 'I love you' – Isle of Ewe/I love you? I find, in life, people generally fall into two categories – those who discover this sort of thing and think, 'Aw, isn't that lovely,' and those who think it may make them puke.

The road then winds its way down the eastern side of Loch Ewe, passing Inverewe Gardens with its enviable selection of subtropical plant life. I've passed it four times now but never been in, and since our passengers were still recovering from the information about

Gruinard, I didn't want to press them – plus, I know nothing about gardening. Just past the picturesque twin villages of Londubh and Poolewe, the road takes a dog-leg to the west where we stopped for lunch in a lay-by overlooking a string of settlements along the banks of Loch Gairloch (the name is interchangeable: Gairloch, Loch Gair, the Gairloch…). There was none of the wind here that plagued us at Altandhu, the sun was out in an almost cloudless sky. As I fried the bacon we should have had at breakfast, a fat bumblebee made its way from one plant to another nearby, and if it weren't for the gang of youths ruining the peace with their shrieks and bellows, it would have been positively bucolic.

At the village of Gairloch, the road turned south past Sheildaig #1 then a bit later westward where eventually it meets the banks of Loch Maree – and what a beautiful loch it is too. It was yet another one of those perfect moments, the water looked good enough to swim in – in actual fact it was freezing. I know because we stopped in a nice looking camping/parking area and dipped a finger in – it was very cold. We skipped – by which I mean threw stones in the water until some people who had obviously been chewing a wasp in their motorhome came out to frown at us. Rhianna, Alastair and others took photos of the imposing mountain on the far side of the water, a Munro called Slioch and a hint of the Torridon Mountains to come – the area we were about to enter.

In truth, most of the hills and mountains since Ullapool could be described as Torridons, as they're all made of the same stuff: a hard and respectably ancient sandstone known as Torridonian Sandstone sitting atop even older Lewisian Gneiss. The Torridons proper however are the peaks found to the north of Glen Torridon (the Glen we were driving through) and within the Torridon Forest – although there are few trees now. Be that as it may, these mountains have a character all of their own. We got a hint of it as we made our way down the length of Loch Maree, but it wasn't until we got to Kinlochewe and turned south and east into Glen Torridon itself and the A896 to Torridon village that the full majesty of the mountains became apparent. I've been here before, but I think you could drive that road repeatedly and never tire of the views – if anyone in our group was bored of the scenery, they were soon yanked out of their torpor. The Torridon Mountains are very distinct and stark, standing as they do on their own and rising from very close to sea level up to well over 3000 ft. The sides are steeply terraced and present an intimidating site, and the peaks are topped with quartzite which gives them a frosted appearance – they really are a site worth seeing. Take Glen Coe, which is no less grand or dangerous than Glen Torridon, with its mountains that are greener so somehow softer, and in a way more familiar so perhaps less intimidating. The Torridon hills are grey and almost other-worldly with their austere peaks and uniformly stepped sides. My words don't do it justice; you should probably go and see for yourself.

The village of Torridon spreads itself out comfortably along the banks of Upper Loch Torridon and it's safe to say it enjoys the most winsome and alluring setting any Scottish village could wish for, sitting at sea level in the midst of some of the most rugged mountains. I don't want to start pining away again, but it's all a bit too beautiful for words. A bit further on past the point where Upper Loch Torridon becomes Loch Sheildaig, we came to the Sheildaig #2 – which should really be Sheildaig #1 because it's definitely the better of the two. I don't want to say too much about the place because it's the kind of place I might retire to; suffice to say, it's an actual village, not a posh hunting lodge like Sheildaig #1. It has a village shop, a pub and hotel, a village campsite which at the time of writing this was free to use (although there are plenty B&Bs) and a postcard perfect sea front setting. It goes without saying, feel free to visit but you can't move there, it's mine.

Perhaps it's just my perception of the place, but Sheildaig to me, represents a gateway of sorts. If you're travelling south as we were, it's the last village that feels properly remote and while it is somewhat geared up for tourism, it doesn't do it in the same way some other villages do – by which I mean in a theme park-like manner. There is an undemanding composure to the place, an agreeable authenticity. Visitors are invited to part with their cash if they so desire, but no one is scrabbling around frantically trying to extract the last euro, dollar or South Korean won from visitors. It still seems to be more a place to live than a place for people to visit – I'm not sure if that makes sense but it's what I like about it. I have no idea what the young people thought, though they seemed to approve of the shop because they denuded it almost entirely of confectionary and energy drinks and left the young man behind the counter quite flustered at the sudden activity.

Back in the minibus, having lost track of what lights were on and what lights were off on the dashboard and now having no idea whether many of them should or shouldn't be on, we left picturesque Sheildaig. If I was you, I'd avoid it, it's not worth the journey, truly…

The road from Sheildaig to Ardarroch cuts across the base of the Applecross peninsula, and shortly before Ardarroch travellers can turn left at a place called Tournapress and experience the Road to Applecross. It's famous in certain circles due to its setting and layout. It climbs from sea level to the Bealach Na Bà pass at a height of 2053ft in at first a series of gentle undulations that culminate in a somewhat hair-raising set of hairpin bends – so much so, we weren't going to try it in our hired minibus. I've been down it on a motorcycle and it had its moments – I mean, it's not the Stelvio Pass, but you definitely want to check your breaks before you start down and I suppose, if you're going up the way, make sure your clutch is in good working order.

From here on we would be returning to a more lived in Scotland. Where before the land had been allowed to get on with things with minimal human involvement, the number of fields, trimmed hedges and landscaped gardens were increasing – we were passing back into a more developed environment. After cutting away from the coast at Ardarroch and over to Lochcarron, the road almost turns back on itself to the north east – indeed, if you stay on that road, you'll end up back in Dingwall on the east coast. We on the other hand turned south again to Strathcarron, Attadale, Ardnarff and Stromeferry (No Ferry).

I should say, Stromeferry (No Ferry) is not its proper name. Stromeferry is a tiny village on the southern banks of Loch Carron (the road signs for the village are mentioned in Iain Banks' book Complicity), and the reason it's appended with the words 'No Ferry' is because there used to be a ferry that cut the corner across Loch Carron, but there isn't anymore. Because confused tourists might think there still is, the signposts are appended with 'No Ferry' in brackets. It's traditional when passing for one traveller to say, 'Stromeferry?' and for another to sadly answer, 'No ferry.' (What can I say, long journeys can be boring.)

And so to Auchtertyre. We were back on a major road, by which I mean an 'A' road with traffic, and although I don't exactly remember, I think it's safe to say we had to wait for some cars to pass before we turned onto the A87, the main road to the isles, and west toward Skye. Before the Isle of Skye though was the town – an actual town, our first since Ullapool – of Kyle of Lochalsh. It is a place that has improved a hundred-fold over the past ten years or so. It was the main ferry terminal for people visiting Skye until the bridge was built, but then suffered something of a decline as cars stopped stopping for the ferry and instead whizzed by on the road. Now though, it's quite nice, or at least we all thought so as we whizzed by in our minibus. Truthfully, I've stopped once or twice in the past and it used to be a bit grey and depressing, but now it has a bit more colour and is a much nicer place to be, assuming you have time to stop.

In order to visit Skye, it used to be that you had to get on a boat – as immortalised by the Skye Boat Song. This is a Scottish folk song with hazy roots, an old highland rowing measure. The words (about Bonnie Prince Charlie after the Jacobite defeat at Culloden in 1746) were written by Sir Harold Boulton and set to an air collected by a lady called Ann Campbelle Macleod who apparently was being rowed over the sea to – well, you get the idea. (She was actually being rowed over an inland loch on the Isle of Skye at the time, but never mind.) It was extremely popular in the late 1800s when it was initially released on iTunes (I'm joking) and enjoyed a number of resurgences as far afield as Australia where it was re-imagined by one Glen Ingram in the 1960s – it's on YouTube although I can't in good conscience compel you to seek it out because it's bloody awful. There was also a version released by Des O'Connor aided and abetted by 'Whistling' George Whittaker... I'm going to check that out now...

Right, there's some time I'm not getting back…

The bridge that replaced the ferry was the source of some unhappiness. Apart from no longer speeding on a bonny boat over the sea to Skye, it wasn't a popular idea at the time because of the way it was being funded. The Skye Bridge was one of the first Private Finance Initiatives in the UK. Not wishing to go into too much detail (my knowledge of PFI is on a par with my knowledge of geology), PFI was a way of financing big infrastructure projects without any upfront funding from the Exchequer. Essentially, a conglomeration of companies bid for the work then run it for a period of time charging the public directly or the Exchequer for the service. It's a way for government to maintain infrastructure development without spending any money up front – sort of. But it's also ruinously expensive. So much so that according to a report in the *Independent* newspaper (April 2015) every man, woman and child in the UK is in debt to the tune £3,400 for PFI – that's over £222 billion owed to the private sector by government on PFI alone. Obviously bridges, hospitals and railways and so on cost money, but take the Skye road bridge as an example; it cost £25 million to build (estimate build cost was £15 million). During the PFI tenure, the company running the bridge (Skye Bridge Ltd – essentially a management shell) took in £33.3 million in tolls with estimated running costs of only £3.5 million and not only that, in 2004, Scottish Transport Minister Nicol Stephen arranged to buy the bridge for £27 million in order to scrap the toll.

So we effectively paid £25 million to build it, but didn't own it, then collectively paid £33.5 million to use it, but still didn't own it, and finally we then had to buy it for £27 million so we *could* own it and scrap the toll fees.

Up until the bridge opening in 1995, Caledonian MacBrayne operated the ferry service and made a good profit each year despite allowing locals to travel for free – not strictly permitted, but many of the staff were local and the summer traffic made up for it. There is a story doing the rounds that when the German football team beat England in a cup game (I'm not sure which, but it's probably easier to just say 'any of them'), the ferry staff allowed cars with German registration plates to travel for free. It is also said that in the first year of the bridge's operation, traffic was a third higher than that reported by Caledonian MacBrayne – make of that what you will.

The problem with the toll was, while it cost 80p to cross the Forth Road Bridge, it cost £11.40 for a return trip on the much shorter bridge to Skye, which made it the most expensive road bridge in the world based on distance travelled. Meanwhile, many other roads and bridges were being built without PFI in the Western Isles, and while they may not have had the scope of the Skye Bridge, there was no charge to use them. Over 500 local people were cited for non-payment of the toll, with 130 being convicted of non-payment. The very first person to be convicted – the secretary of the Skye Bridge Anti Toll protest group – spent a short time in prison for non-payment.

It's all settled down now of course, and it's free to cross the bridge. Well I say that – we are all still paying off the debt accrued on our behalf.

You could write a whole book about the Isle of Skye: from the dramatic Black Cuillin Ridge, from which the rest of the island and its smaller satellite islands seem to radiate, to Dunvegan Castle, the seat of the Clan MacLeod. Then there are MacLeod's Tables – two distinctive flat-topped hills in the far west of the island. The Black Cuillin Ridge boasts twelve Munro tops, including the only Munro that requires mountaineering skills to reach – Sgurr Dearg (the Red Peak). It's topped with what is known as the Inaccessible Pinnacle (or the In Pin). This Munro was said not to have been completed by Sir Hugh Munro (he who first collated the list of mountains rising to 3000ft or more) because he didn't do the In Pin. It's all a bit moot because he missed others over 3000ft (or 912 metres) too. The Reverand Archibald Eneas Robertson was said to be the first to 'bag' all of the Munros in 1901, but even he turned back due to adverse weather on Ben Wyvis and also didn't do the In Pin because, at the time, it wasn't on Sir Hugh's list. I don't know about you, but it comes as a huge shock to me that there are those who might lie about their adventures in the great outdoors, that they might prop up youth hostel reception desks and tell fibs about their escapades while they fiddle with all the zips on their walking trousers…

In truth, we were only on Skye so we could say we'd taken in a Scottish Island on our tour. Unfortunately, we didn't manage to explore any of it, since by the time we hove-to in our wheezy chuffing minibus, it was getting on for teatime. We'd booked a hostel back at the lay-by overlooking Gairloch, and it was a bit of a gamble because all we had was a number we'd found during a stilted web search on a smart phone in the Tesco car park in Ullapool. As I've said before, it can be a high risk strategy booking into an unknown hostel – anything could happen, from having to make small talk with a Dutch murderer to having to share a room with people who might have leprosy, or worse still, snore.

This hostel, called Broadford Backpackers Hostel, looked okay though. The building used to be a health centre – I know that because there were emergency call buttons on the walls of the rooms and a bathroom with the tub right in the middle of the room (easy access for care staff and hoists). I suspect the management thought they could make the bathroom a bit less austere by placing candles around the room and quirky art work on the walls; however, the impression I got was that people may have been bathed against their will in there. We managed to get the Explorer Scouts booked into a room by themselves, while myself and Leaders Number Two and Three booked a four-bed room so we wouldn't find ourselves sharing with an axe murderer or other 'lone travellers'. (I don't know what it is about hostels. I just think they're probably frequented by murderers on the run from European Arrest Warrants.) If I had to choose between Broadford Backpackers and Sandra's back in Thurso, I'd choose Sandra's. The Health Centre Hostel (which is how I'm going to refer to it) was everything that is disagreeable about hostels whereas Sandra's was just endearingly naff. At Sandra's, the owners seemed surprised we'd chosen to stay there, at the Health Centre Hostel we were accepted in like raw material at the beginning of an assembly line – I felt as if we'd been processed. Sandra's never asked for everyone's name, address and email, whereas the Health Centre did, and more (they would have taken our passports if we'd had them). The other customers we saw at Sandra's at least smiled; at The Health Centre they mostly scowled suspiciously, and it seemed to be everyone for themselves during dinner – inmates were sitting with one arm round their plates staring warily around, presumably to keep others from stealing their food.

That said, I still believe there is no such thing as a bad experience. The Health Centre Hostel had its charms – we just needed to look a bit harder to find them. Being strictly fair, apart from a mismatch in terms of the number of people it could put up versus the number of people who could cook a meal then sit down and eat it (the kitchen and dining room were far too small), it's really the clientele who need to cheer up. It shouldn't need to be said, but I will, just in case, our group was a shining example. You've been along the road with us this far and you'd have to agree, we're a delightful bunch, diffident, polite and mindful of people around us, regardless of how mindless they might be around us. Truly, we're a joy to be around...

It's a well known fact that Spanish people (for example) don't know what a queue is, while British people are somewhat infatuated with the concept, and I think it's safe to say both the Spanish and British peoples would accept this analysis. So there is an inevitable clash of cultures when a lot of perhaps not particularly assertive young Scots are trying to cook a stir fry, and then several Spaniards with pointy elbows and bulldozer hips take our decision to cook dinner as a cue to do the same. Our group of youngsters didn't stand a chance – they didn't have to go far from the hob before some handsome bronzed devil would simply move their pan aside and put theirs in its place. The Spanish contingent required a crash course in waiting their turn, which Leader Number Two and I were forced to provide. Normally, I'd be the first to admit most people will beat me in the kitchen, but not that evening, Scottish pride was at stake.

The dining arrangements were also a bit challenging. With space for only twenty to sit down at any one time (given the hostel slept 38 in total and it was full) and having to slot in with already seated groups of scowling Europeans, it wasn't exactly a relaxed dining experience after the gauntlet that was the kitchen. Two tables were fully occupied by chatting groups (they may have been French), and a third table had a German fellow in attendance. Where Spaniards have no concept of a decent queue, Germans have no concept of fashion. Even with my standards, I could stand next to an average German hostel user and look like I'd been styled by Gok Wan. He was wearing a vivid lime-green tracksuit and had staked his claim to the table with a huge stainless steel pot of tea, his jacket on one chair and a multi-pack of Wotsits on another, he'd laid down his territory well. His tracksuit became for the rest of the camp the outfit to which all others were compared – we talk about it even now.

The last two tables had been pushed together end to end and an effortlessly good looking couple from one of the Scandinavian countries had set up camp, not at one end of the table, but right in the middle. It is tempting to capitalise the last four words of the previous sentence – I mean I don't think I have OCD, but why would anyone do that? They came in and sat opposite each other in the middle of the table. I suppose we could have put towels down or something, but they clocked us making for the table, ignored the Lime Green Man's jacket and Wotsits and sat IN THE MIDDLE of the table for eight. We had no choice but to sit around them. I know what you're thinking: 'It's a hostel, make friends, it's supposed to be happy with easy going people living cheek by jowl…' But has anyone ever stayed in a hostel like that? Everyone is suspicious of everyone else. There is no free love or people exchanging email addresses or Instagrams or whatever it is people do these days. It's just a bunch of flinty-eyed, slightly skint Europeans regarding each other with equal parts disdain and distrust with a slight undertone of mortification because they couldn't afford to stay in a hotel.

Anyway, I don't wish to do down the Health Centre Hostel. The people running it had tried, with quirky artwork on the walls, ample showers (although the lights kept turning off – it was like being in the womb again, which some may find pleasant) and a useful setting on the outskirts of Broadford. It was just difficult to get a sense of the place because it was a bit impersonal with an alarming proliferation of stark warning notices about what not to do and when things would close. It reminded me of the TV adverts big banks and utility companies favour: they get folksy artists with whimsically trilling voices to write quirky songs on a ukulele then use it as a soundtrack for a quaint animated story about a cute rabbit or loveable cow trying to buy a house. Hardly anyone is fooled though; the advert is for a grasping transnational capitalist entity that wouldn't piss on you if you were on fire.

I'm not saying the Health Centre Hostel was like that; I think a better analogy might be a one night stand (I am now officially on a tangent). Imagine if you can going on a date. It seems like a good idea so long as you don't scrutinise it too closely. You meet and neither of you immediately disregards the other; instead, you find each other agreeable enough to the extent you're prepared to see where things go. You have some dinner and perhaps some wine, and as the wine goes down so do the inhibitions. You might have coffee after dinner, then go to a quiet place for several more drinks – for courage you understand. Before you know it you're back at their place and while, on some level, you both know what is about to transpire could be a source of future regret, both of you are resigned to the fact some reciprocal itch scratching (so to speak) is going to take place, which at this late stage is unavoidable because you spent all your cash on wine and beer and the last bus departed some time ago. The analogy I'm desperately trying to draw here is the night before, they seemed quite into you, they wanted you – needed you even. But come the morning, whilst you feel slightly dirty in an unidentifiable way, it's also blatantly obvious they want you off their property. They'll be hovering at the end of the bed waiting to strip the sheets, or fidgeting with your smart going-out-on-the-town-jacket by the front door.

The Health Centre Hostel was a bit like that.

Day Seven – Broadford to Loch Ness (again)

The iconic Eilean Donan Castle on the road back from Skye

It was Friday morning, our last full day on the road. Usually by this time, attendees are looking forward to going home to their own beds. If we were camping for the week, we'd be spending the day tidying up, which is without doubt the most depressing part of a good Scout camp. Even though we may not have washed properly for a week, or the kids might have been horrible, or the camp bed that felt so rustic and novel at the beginning of the week now felt like a medieval torture device, if it's been a good summer camp (despite being a bit smelly, having back pain or feeling mentally bruised) having to break camp and go home is a cruel drudge.

If you're only staying for one night, there's not much point in getting too comfortable, but if you're going to be there for a week, it makes sense – although it takes a lot of gear to be truly comfortable, it is worth it. Let me tell you about a typical summer camp for our Scout troop. Our group has changed slightly due to leaders moving on (we're a bit more 'lightweight' these days) but not so long ago, we were the kings of heavyweight camping. Our main meeting place during camp would be a 40 × 20 foot marquee with a 12 × 12 foot cook tent tacked onto one end. There would be a table tennis table for eating, activities and of course the Summer Camp Table Tennis Championships (which I invariably lost). Our cook tent would be ringed by heavy duty wooden tables topped with various gas cookers, urns and ovens along with storage for food, pots and pans, and other sundry items – and the floor would be carpeted. The main marquee was never carpeted – I mean, we weren't completely mad, but there is something to be said about being in a tent but on a carpet. I should say, some leaders (usually later on in the evening) could be found enjoying the novel experience of lying flat on their backs on a carpet in a field while looking at canvas above their head. This was never a daytime activity because leaders would be a lot more cognisant of the carpet's origins – usually the Scout's bi-annual jumble sale. We weren't fussy, but during lean years, often it was preferable to lie on the ground than on the carpets we had donated to our jumble sales. In any case, some years we enjoyed luxurious shag pile rugs in the cook tent whilst in other years, the floor covering was more spartan. The kids would be in Icelandic II type tents, heavy-duty patrol tents 16 ft long and 8 ft wide in which it was possible to stand (no need to get dressed while lying down). Inhabitants could wrestle, crawl around or lean on the centre upright when putting socks on and – there is no delicate way to say this, so I'll just say it – pee outside the tent without unlacing the doors. Of course, care had to be taken not to pee on any shoes left outside, but it was very much the responsibility of the shoes' owners to ensure this didn't happen. If it did, then it was the cause of great hilarity for those looking on while the shoe owner tried to convince themselves the dampness they felt creeping between their toes was just fresh morning dew. Anyway, Icelandic tents had no sewn-in groundsheet, so separate heavy-duty tarpaulins were brought for flooring, and for extra weather proofing, a fly sheet (essentially a second tent) was pitched over the first one thus doubling the total weight. If pitched incorrectly, they were drafty, hard to keep warm and prone to leaks, but were still infinitely better than the benighted, claustrophobic hike tents we use today.

None of the above was an issue for us though. We showered, brushed our teeth and packed our bags, manhandled sleeping bags into stuff-sacks, got our coats from fidgeting hostel staff, then stood outside for half an hour waiting for the remainder of our group to finish their morning ablutions. I think anyone who has children of a certain age will be familiar with this phenomenon: the adolescent child's love/hate relationship with the beauty and cleansing process. Some take it far too seriously while others don't take it seriously at all. Sometimes a young person can refrain from bathing for days on end with no noticeable change in circumstance, and then there are some who could melt chevrons off the road at twenty paces with their armpits. There is a line which is as palpable as any physical barrier beyond which bathing is an essential part of the daily routine and some of our group were determined not to cross it and for that I thank them. Not that they smell or anything, I don't think any of them do. What I mean to say is, I don't check – sometimes we drop hints, or throw a can of lynx at a person, but we don't sniff test them as such.

Eventually, with the minibus packed and its fragrant passengers sitting in a haze of deodorant and hair mousse, we made off into the day. There were no new lights on the dashboard, or at least none that we could identify. The van was slightly lighter today than it was yesterday because the previous evening we decided to gift the Broadford Backpackers Hostel the box of couscous we'd been given at Sandra's. I know, some of you may feel it was far too generous, and on the off chance any of the hostel staff felt the same way, we left it at the back of a cupboard and kept quiet about our benevolence. Truly, it's just the kind of people we are.

I know this might seem unusual given the rest of this book, but if I could impart a rare tip to those travelling in the area...if you want to tell friends and family you've been on an island hopping holiday, from Broadford, turn south on the A851 to Armadale, where you can get an inexpensive ferry to Mallaig. From Mallaig (which is a nice coastal town, so worth a visit) you can either head straight for Fort William via Glenfinnan and its famous viaduct, or turn south at Lochailort (about 20 miles before Glenfinnan). If you do turn south, you'll pass through yet more classic Scottish scenery: Roshven, Kinlochmoidart and Acharacle (another great Scottish place name.) Eventually, at Salen you can veer westward toward the Ardnamurchan Peninsula and the most westerly point on mainland Britain. It's a hell of a road in (reminiscent of the road to Altandhu) and a dead end to boot, but it's well worth it – it's quite rugged (wild stags come right up to the road to look at you as you pass) and the Ardnamurchan lighthouse and museum is worth a look, assuming you catch it while open. We managed to do just that while on our motorcycle tour. It had a charmingly naff display on what sound best carries through air and water. There was a button marked 'cow moo' and sure enough, when pressed a deep sonorous 'moo' emanated from hidden speakers. (Apparently a cow's moo carries well under water – good for communication, although not so good for the cow.) There were other buttons for whale song, an oboe and a piccolo, but none of those came close to the deep mournful song of the cow. It was such a sad sound, full of regret and sorrow, possibly because at the time the cow was being forced to moo under water.

From Ardnamurchan and its unfortunate recording of the cow being drowned, it's a long road back to Ardgour and the Corran Ferry which eventually takes you to the A82 just south of Fort William – the only downside to that route is missing Glenfinnan to the north.

On its way to Ardgour, the road also passes through a village called Strontian which may sound familiar to comic fans. The mineral strontianite from which the chemical element strontium comes (chemical symbol, Sr, atomic number, 38, if you're interested) was mined in the hills above the settlement. Strontium Dog was the name of a comic strip popular in the 1980s – or at least it was when it was in my *2000 AD* annual. Agents of the Search/Destroy Agency – bounty hunters in a post-apocalyptic world drenched in radioactive strontium 90 – wore a badge with 'SD' (the agency's initials) emblazoned on, which gave rise to the nickname Strontium Dogs. Mock if you will, but Johnny Alpha, one of the most famous Strontium Dogs brought Adolf Hitler into the future to pay for his crimes. He also donated a lot of cash to Milton Keynes (Johnny Alpha, not Adolf Hitler), which in his post-nuclear holocaust world is a giant ghetto – make of that what you will. I still have my *2000 AD* annual and I bet it would be worth real money if I hadn't completed the Judge Dredd word search and maze in blue biro…

But I digress again…

Unfortunately, putting a minibus on a ferry is an expensive endeavour, so we returned the way we came over the Skye Bridge. We headed back inland toward Fort William where we were due to meet Ally's parents, who were on their way to their cottage near to our new favourite campsite back at Altandhu.

As you might imagine, it doesn't matter what route you take through that part of Scotland as there's always something to look at – and Eilean Donan Castle is certainly something. It's one of Scotland's most iconic buildings, and even in silhouette, it is readily identifiable. The castle as it is today is a relatively modern building, completed as it was in the 1930s. It had lain in ruins since it was destroyed during the Jacobite uprising of 1719. In the time up to 1719, its occupants spent a lot of time killing each other or people who happened by, or were killed by people who happened by. Habitation on the island is thought to date as far back as the 6th century when an early Christian monastic cell existed on the island. Although no evidence of these buildings survive today, people who know about these things believe it was dedicated to Saint Donan of Eigg. Donan was a Gaelic priest probably over from Ireland to convert the local Picts – it didn't go well. He was martyred and later became the patron saint of the Isle of Eigg. Apparently, Donan was the abbot of a monastery on the Isle of Eigg when according to Michael O'Clery's *The Martyrology of Donegal* (a 17th century compilation and rip-roaring read) robbers landed on the island during mass, whereupon Donan beseeched the robbers not to kill anyone until after the mass had finished. The invaders did pause – presumably to sharpen their weapons – then proceeded to chop the heads off Donan and 52 of his monks. I think we can all agree and, as Roy Castle often said, that's dedication. Eilean Donan translated means Isle of Donan, so the unfortunate priest is at least remembered by the millions of shortbread tins, calendars and postcards tourists cart away with them after visiting.

Most people will be familiar with the TV programme *Time Team*, the show in which Tony Robinson would caper energetically round a hill or field? As he did that, various grizzly men, winsome lady archaeologists and nerds with ground-penetrating radar would burrow into local history and the ground to unearth snippets of ancient information. Tony would go into conniptions over a pottery shard found in a 'ditch' (so much of that program seemed to revolve around clever people rummaging through ancient garbage) then become euphoric at the opening of another trench. I only mention it because in a thousand years' time, I wonder if there will be another version of *Time Team* beamed to Holo-Cubes™ or Personal Virtual Reality Zones™. These future people will be watching a 30th century equivalent of Tony Robinson having a moment because a robot (probably) uncovered evidence of a gift shop and café: 'Yes TonyBot 3000, this is a fascinating find. It's an early 21st century key ring and bottle opener…and we've also found evidence of tea towels…'

Eilean Donan is a well visited attraction and served to remind us we were very much back in the main drag of Scottish tourism. October is a lot less busy than June or July, but there's still a fair bit of tourist traffic, usually camper vans with the odd coach party thrown in to really hold people up. We parked the bus in a capacious and mostly empty parking area and considered going into the castle. The price however proved to be just over the threshold of acceptability, so instead, we just enjoyed the views across the water toward the castle and the village of Dornie. Obviously these days you don't have to actually visit a place because through the medium of TripAdvisor, you can pay a visit vicariously. Overall it gets good ratings, but among the terrible/poor/average comments, the most common complaint seemed to be its age, or lack thereof. Since it was rebuilt between 1913 and 1932, it's not a medieval castle as such, but a lot of people don't realise this so are disappointed by its lack of antiquity internally. Which is something of a shame I suppose, so perhaps – as we did – it's best photographed from the car park. After group photographs in various heroic poses were taken with the castle as a backdrop, we moved on.

Past Inverinate, Morvich and Shiel Bridge, the road takes you into the shadow of the Five Sisters of Kintail – five mountain peaks all over 3000ft with three qualifying as Munros. You may ask why, if they're all over 3000ft, are all five not Munros. Well, when Sir Hugh Munro set about compiling his list of mountains, he didn't lay down any parameters for what constituted a separate mountain top. Most mountains sit in among other mountains in ranges or ridges, and it's sometimes difficult to know where one ends and the next begins. Occasionally the list changes to reflect new thinking and even now, mountains that were hitherto thought to be over 3000ft have been found to be lacking the vital few inches, so have been downgraded to a Corbett. A Corbett by the way, is a hill 2500ft to 3000ft in height with an ascent of at least 500ft to each peak, to say they've been downgraded is a unfair really, because they are often just as challenging to conquer. I haven't been up a Munro in years and I didn't get as far as the Kintail ridge, and although looking up at the peaks from the road is pleasant, it is not as satisfying as looking down at the road from the peaks. It is a source of real regret that I no longer do any walking; unfortunately, a love of wine and pies has taken hold – just writing about it has left me breathless.

The road took us along the northern banks of Loch Cluanie, a reservoir of water held behind the Cluanie dam for the purpose of electricity generation, and which is also quite nice to look at. The road splits in two at a place called Bun Loyne but both routes terminate back in the Great Glen – we took the road to the west and Invergarry and eventually Fort William. I'd argue it's the nicer of the two roads, taking in as it does Loch Loyne and Loch Garry; the latter is particularly nice to look at in the mid-morning sunshine, so much so, we stopped to take a group photo. I was going to say arriving in the village of Invergarry was something of a milestone, but of course it wasn't really. The route of the Great Glen Way that our group had traversed only last Monday passes along the opposite side of Loch Oich. The proper milestone was where the Great Glen Way bisects the A82 at the entrance to the Great Glen Water Park at Laggan. As we trundled past, it didn't feel like the last time we were there was Monday of the same week.

So we were back on familiar territory with no plans for that evening's accommodation. We thought we might have a final night at Laggan or perhaps Gairlochy on one of the British Waterways campsites, but Lewis and I had hatched a plan which we'll get to later. Our next stop was the Nevis Range Mountain Resort. I'm the last person to do down Scottish tourism, but it sounds a lot grander than it really is. Which is not to say it's crap. It's certainly as intimidating as any other centre for mildly dangerous outdoor pursuits. There was no snow on the ground but the mountain bike runs and cable car were open, and it was to the latter our group turned for the morning's entertainment. I've been on the cable car before and if I'm being honest, I didn't enjoy it on account of my complete cowardice when it comes to heights. I was at Alton Towers a good few years ago, although I can't remember or imagine the reason I was there, but there I was with some friends. The first ride we took was indoors, and I remember at the time thinking, 'How awful could it be – it's indoors?' Well, very as it turned out. We were made to sit astride a motorcycle-like contraption, then wedged firmly in by safety apparatus (forcing a most un-Victorian level of intimacy with other thrill-seekers) and off we went into the dark.

From memory (most of which I've blocked out) it was called the *Corkscrew* or the *Black Hole* – I don't remember which. I'm not a fan of roller coasters, but I thought since this one was indoors, it would be quite tame. It probably was by other people's standards, so all I'll say is it didn't agree with me. I genuinely don't get the compunction to do that to yourself; I mean, why? As I stumbled away from the ride wiping spittle from my chin, I vowed not to go on another roller coaster and didn't. I did go on the cable car ride and found that to be terrifying in more insidious ways; instead of the quick horror of the roller coaster, the brevity of which doesn't really allow time to contemplate the many horrid ways you might die, the cable car just dangles you high up in the air for twenty minutes stopping every now and again for no reason other than to swing gently from side to side or back and forth. It allows you plenty of time to imagine what might happen if the cable snaps or some other vital component decides to give way. Suffice to say, I spent the rest of my day at Alton Towers with feet firmly on the ground. The most thrilling things got after that was being chased away from bins by gangs of wasps. Hard as it might be to believe, given all my other anxieties, wasps don't bother me. While on Scout camp in Ireland, one flew up the sleeve of my T-shirt and stung me. I don't recall running around shrieking and flailing my arms, although I do accept it was a long time ago and nostalgia can be an enthusiastic editor of memory. Interestingly (or not, probably not), the Victorian sensibilities that mean I prefer not to spoon with strangers on indoor roller coasters, also mean that it is most unseemly to run away from wasps. I have no idea what any of that means from an existential point of view or in terms of character beyond a vague notion that it may make me seem quite stupid.

Anyway, the point was, I sent our Explorers (along with Leaders Number Two and Three) up the cable car (I think the operators prefer to call it a gondola). I sat with an expensive cup of coffee and watched ultra-sporty people crash down the side of the hill on mountain bikes while more timid examples pootled around the car park or attempted to complete the beginner's course just outside the café.

The Nevis Range is quite impressive really, and it's done a pretty good job of diversifying: in the winter (assuming the snow fall is good) it gets the skiing crowd, and then out with the ski season, it gets the mountain bike crowd. There are a number of mountain bike tracks to choose from (bear in mind I know nothing about these things): green runs (easy), blue runs (not so easy) and red runs (suicidal). There are also 'jump lines'. It took me a few minutes to realise what a jump line actually was – it's a downhill course with ramps and humps. I was rather hoping participants started a jump line by exiting a cable car from an unspecified height astride a mountain bike onto the track. I was going to chastise myself for being silly, but as I sat with my coffee watching windswept and interesting people tumble down the side of the hill on their pushbikes, it really didn't seem that far fetched.

Eventually my intrepid Explorers returned fresh-faced from their mountainside adventure. No cable cars plunged to the ground and no one decided to re-enact any scenes from *Where Eagles Dare*. We pondered having a go on the recently opened high ropes course but saw the price so had to say no. Anyway, we had an appointment to keep on behalf of Ally – his parents were on their way to Fort William so we needed to be too.

Inverness markets itself as the Highland Capital, whereas Fort William tells all interested parties it is the Outdoor Capital of Scotland. I can't really argue with that, and going in at Inverness and coming out at Fort William is a fine way to circumnavigate the north of Scotland. However, if I can make a suggestion, if you're going to travel around Scotland but not going to walk any of the Great Glen Way, start in Perth. From there, take the A93 past Scone Palace and Guildtown. I would recommend that road for a number of reasons, not least that it takes you past the Meikleour Beach Hedge – the tallest hedge in the world. Planted in 1745, as you approach, it's not immediately obvious what you're seeing, but then as you round a gentle bend in the road, people with you will start to say things like, 'HOLY GUACAMOLE! Is that really a hedge?' It was planted by men who were called to fight in the Jacobite rebellion, none of whom survived. It was then left to grow in their memory, or so the story goes. These days it's trimmed and re-measured every ten years, there is an information board at its southern end which is worth reading, if you're into your hedges that is.

But I digress. We were approaching Fort William, a business-like town and a roiling mass of zip pocketed 'outdooristas' (a word I've just made up.) At any given time, the number of activity trouser pockets in Fort William can outnumber the number of people by as many as 10,000 to 1, although it's also true to say, this may be another thing I'm making up. I like it though – it's a lively place. I especially like that many of the locals couldn't give a shit about the famous mountain under which they live or that they live in the Outdoor Capital of Scotland. I think it might be a belligerent streak in the local population. They don't go mountain biking, skiing, snow boarding, line jumping or ice climbing. They do their make up, wear senselessly impractical footwear and clothes from Next, River Island or Top Man and get steaming drunk and eat kebabs at the weekend.

The expectation in a place as immersed and surrounded by the great outdoors as Fort William is that everyone will be going to do or coming back from doing outdoor activities. While it's certainly true most of the visitors are there for vigorous bouts of outdoor shenanigans (although the town also caters to many coach parties of OAPs). It's just nice that a lot of the locals don't really care about it. When you go into an outdoor equipment retailer, you expect the staff to be ardent outdoorists – if they aren't, then you can pretend you are, which is always a novelty. So it is in places like Fort William, that there is a similar expectation, and one that is smashed to pieces if you happen to be there at chucking out time (for example) on a Friday or Saturday night – there is a substantial sliver of Fort William's inhabitants who enjoy a drink. During the day though, it's quite nice, there is a handsome pedestrianised main drag with a good selection of shops selling various tourist paraphernalia. You can for example buy a towel that is a kilt/that is a towel (it's a tartan towel), or many varieties of tinned shortbread, whisky miniatures or Scottish themed tea towels. There's a great wee shop that still manages to sell all sorts of offensive items: BB guns, pen knifes, daggers and swords. These are always a big draw on Scout camp, especially for the kids. Back in the day (in my case, the 80s) at summer camp, we'd have half a day to wander about the nearest sizeable town. Back then most towns had two types of outdoor/rural pursuit outlets that had dangerous items for sale. The first was always too posh – it sold shot guns and Barbour jackets. The other was a seedier establishment. It didn't sell shotguns because the proprietor (usually a small furtive man) wasn't allowed a licence. Instead they sold GAT guns, BB guns, Black Widow or the much sought after Diablo catapults and crossbows, pen knifes, sheath knifes, flick knifes, butterfly knifes, fireworks all year round, and fishing tackle for a veneer of respectability. For a group of 12-year-old boys in 1985 with an unusual amount of money in their grubby hands, it was better than a sweetie shop. Not any more though. Now-a-days the most dangerous thing a Scout might buy is a Bic lighter, and when it comes to outright offence, the canny child opts for a copy of *Nutz* magazine.

We were due to liaise with Ally's parents outside Fort William's main supermarket; and so it was we found their car, weighed down by bikes, luggage and Ally's twin sister - and shortly thereafter found his Mum to whom we gracefully passed the duty of care. Ally had been a constant source of amusement during the trip, and as he pulled away in his parents heavily laden car, his weeping face pressed against a window, an unusual silence descended upon the group. Ally likes to talk, and is to silence what nature is to a vacuum. We twiddled our thumbs and gently un-popped our ears then went into the superstore for what was our last resupply of the trip.

Since we were in the Outdoor Capital of Scotland, we thought we might do something vaguely outdoorsy, so we reboarded the bus and headed out of Fort William and up Glen Nevis. This is the road you'd take if you were going to take the tourist route up Ben Nevis; it's also the finishing stretch of the West Highland Way. We trundled past a steady flow of bedraggled walkers who'd just made their way along the glen that links Kinlochleven and Lairig Mor then over the much gentler southern ridge of Glen Nevis itself – the views of Ben Nevis from which are some of the best. It was a clear day, so looking to our left, we could trace the route of the tourist path as it zigzagged up the side of Ben Nevis, the top of which is hidden by the bulk of the mountain itself. We had to slow down considerably as we passed the Glen Nevis Youth Hostel – to give the finger to any smug outdooristas standing at reception wearing body warmers, trousers with too many zips and smug expressions on their face. Plus the road narrows drastically, and in a minibus filled with other people's children, it's necessary to take care.

The road in is almost as interesting as the scenery through which it passes; blind corners and summits not-with-standing, the surroundings make it a worthwhile drive. With dashboard lights all a-flicker and brake discs gently glowing, we arrived at the car park which is the start of many high level walks in the Mamore Mountains. Situated between Glen Nevis and Kinlochleven, the popular Ring of Steall, formed by a group of five Munros that tower above, is a popular route among walkers with ridges branching off to yet more impressive peaks in the range. We made our way on foot along the gorge carved out by the Water of Nevis (it doesn't become the River Nevis until further down the valley at a place near Achriabhach.) The gorge is precipitous in places, and care is required here and there on the path, but eventually we were rewarded with stunning views of the Steall falls – the second highest in Scotland with a single drop of 120 metres (390ft). It's one of the more memorable walks in Scotland, mostly to do with how the falls reveal themselves. You emerge all at once into this quite beautiful hidden flat bottomed glacial valley with the falls as a backdrop. It is without doubt one of the nicest places to visit in Scotland, and it won't cost you a penny.

The group with the Steel Falls in the background

The falls feed the Waters of Nevis, over which there is a wire bridge. I've been here several times under various circumstances and on one occasion I ended up thigh deep (just the one leg) in a bog because I decided not to use the wire bridge. It was August and as I half-sat half-stood trapped in this bog, I could see people in the distance – I really didn't want to have to shout for help but I seemed to be quite stuck. Eventually after a lot of rocking back and forth, cursing, swearing and tears, I managed to extract my leg from the earth's cold clammy grip. Later on whilst fording the Steall Burn, I went hip deep in that too, which was fine really, because it meant the leg that had been immersed in the bog got a wash. It was one of the most ignominious starts to a day's walking I'd ever had. Be that as it may standing here years later, as we stood in the sun watching Explorers edge their way over the wire bridge, we agreed the setting was as close to perfection as we'd seen – peaceful, quiet and eminently bucolic. If you keep on walking you'll eventually find yourself on Rannoch Moor – it's a true wilderness – then the next thing you'll hit is Corrour Station and even then, only if you're lucky.

Once our Explorers were all on the other side of the river, a group of Russian tourists turned up. I say turned up; they bounded up in that way only incredibly fit people do. By this point it was quite busy, and there was a queue for the wire bridge. Most people were going over and coming straight back whilst others where going to the base of the falls to take pictures or to climb hills – the Russians on the other hand wanted to do acrobatics. We watched (I'm not going to say enviously) as one particularly svelte specimen edged his way out, gripped the left hand guide rope with both hands then began what I think can only be described as a 'gymnastic routine'. He swung this way and that, and hoisted himself up; I don't think he did a handstand but it's hard to be sure. I used to be a lot fitter than I am now, but I was never that fit, not even close. Lewis, Michael and I looked at each other then back at the guy, who was now doing one-armed pull ups. Meanwhile our Explorers were looking on from the wrong side of the river. (I could tell by the way they were poised that on their return they had routines of their own to perform that would make the Russians think again…) However, before another Russian athlete could begin a new routine, I approached and asked if I could get my group back first. He acquiesced and asked if I was an outdoor instructor or warden, which I thought was charitable of him – to look at me you wouldn't assume I had an outdoor job. I said no and explained we were Scouts on our annual trip, then complimented him on his physique. I thought about asking him for an ashtray as it's one of the few Russian phrases I remember from lessons taken long ago, but I doubt he was a smoker. Once we had everyone back on the right side of the river, we watched more feats of physical poise, strength and agility, but I felt a stitch coming on so we left. Later, we agreed that we could have replied to the Russian gymnastics with some perturbations of our own, but it would have been petty. We also agreed it would have been more entertaining if one of them had fallen in the river. No one said so out loud, but I think we all thought if they had, they would have emerged from the water (probably in high definition slow motion) with T-shirts clinging to rippling torsos, one playfully wrestling with a bear while the other held a struggling salmon between his teeth. Since they were a good-natured bunch, we would have applauded enthusiastically all the same.

The wire bridge over the Waters of Nevis

The wire bridge was the last significant activity of our trip. We were now officially winding down - we had one more night then the drive home. Depending on how a trip has gone, getting to the end can either be a relief or a disappointment. We'd covered many miles and as I've said, we may have taken on too much, but as we approached our final night together, there was a sense of content in the group. It was getting on for late afternoon and we still didn't have our final night's accommodation booked, so we returned to Fort William and pondered our options. We could return to one of the British Waterways campsites or we could try for something indoors. In the end, while the Explorers were out attempting to procure swords and crossbows from the small shop on Fort William's High Street, I phoned the microcabins back at the Loch Ness Holiday Park and managed to book the same cabins we had earlier in the week. We didn't really have the budget for it, but Lewis and I decided to 'go halfs' as it were, as we really didn't want our last night to be in hike tents. When our Explorers returned – armed to the teeth, we headed back along the Great Glen, eventually pulling in at the Loch Ness Holiday Park. I went into the reception under the ruse of asking if they had any vacancies, but instead picked up keys to the cabins we'd booked. Balefully I returned to the van and told them the bad news, then drove down and parked next to our home for the night to choruses of, 'Yeah, yeah, we knew that was going to happen…'

The evening passed peacefully; we had dinner, played cards and Leader Number Three held court on the small veranda of our microcabin. It's safe to say our Scout group – like most others – has always been a haven for the dispossessed. There is a degree of stigma attached to membership which means the trendiest people tend not to count among our numbers, and that's fine by me. I came all the way up through the sections, was crap at football and paid little attention to the labels my clothes had or how many stripes adorned the sides of my trainers, and it's much the same now. I think young people might appreciate time away from the adolescent rat race; school can be a bruising experience if it's collective conscience decides one of its numbers isn't ticking all the right boxes. Although compliments should be taken in context – I'm as deeply unfashionable now as I was in the 1980s – I would say to Explorers who took this trip, don't ever change, don't ever feel the need to comply or blend in, ignore anyone who tries to insist you're not towing the line because you don't Snapchat, WhatsApp or Instagram, or wear hipster jeans, beanie hats or guy liner – just keep being yourself. If Harry wants to put brown sauce on his cornflake roll, I think that's fine; if John-Andrew wants to bring along his dressing gown and slippers to camp – also fine; if George will only ever wear shorts, even in the dead of winter – okay; and if Rhianna is fine being the only girl among the boys, then why not? Being in Scouts is a great way to put two fingers up to adolescent convention, and I can't think of a better thing to be doing than not being part of the painfully fashionable, perennially paranoid trendy set who fancy themselves as barometers of acceptability among teenagers today. They can take their plucked eyebrows, fashion sense and fear of Wifi dead zones and bugger off. The moment that type of blind obedience to faddy affectation and surrender to brainless celeb-driven conformity invades Scouts is the moment it'll die – and they look down their noses at us…

I don't quite know how we got on to that topic by way of Michael holding court outside the leader's microcabin. He'd be the first to admit he's not a dedicated follower of fashion, but he's not completely without a sense of élan – although do bear in mind, all compliments should be taken in context.

Our final night was quiet; we were all tired due to it being a busy day and the culmination of a week on the road. Being the trendsetters we naturally are, the route we took now has a name and is being touted by Visit Scotland – the NC500, Scotland's answer to Route 66. Hundreds of motorcyclists hurl themselves round the route every summer and no doubt coach parties of Koreans, Japanese and large Americans will be trundling round in years to come. Will the increase in traffic ruin it? Only time will tell. Even now in the peak summer months, residents in villages that used to be havens of peace and tranquillity have to dodge traffic as they cross the road. The flip side is the money the traffic will bring, although arguably, since you could conceivably do it in a day, it may not be worth as much for local business as they hope. Perhaps it'll go the way of the Great Glen and become a theme park of sorts. We don't really eat a lot of shortbread in Scotland, at least, not any more than residents of any other country do, and we don't often prance up and down glens and moors lopping the heads off people who displease us, or cast mysterious spells on our enemies any more. Many of the accents you hear up and down the Great Glen (for example) won't be Scottish – is that a bad thing? No. Is it a thing at all? I don't really know.

I just know it would be a shame if the wilderness between Durness and Ullapool was blighted by traffic and ever more people. If you've been anywhere in the Lake District, which is really very nice indeed, seeing double yellow lines and traffic lights in the middle of nowhere is uniquely depressing. Mind you, Cocoa Mountain making a killing selling their chocolates to coach parties of tourists can only be good for the area – although perhaps not for travellers staring slackly out of bus windows, oblivious to the trademark scenery because they're worried about how they'll get to the end of the month with only a few squares of expensive chocolates to their name. I worry that hundreds of dafties on motorbikes haring round Loch Eriboll will ruin the peace and quiet, and thousands of cars filled with feckless tourists will leave a trail of litter the length of the Torridon Mountains. I like people, I really do, but sometimes we're not very responsible. Perhaps if I said it was terrible, a bland featureless slog marked only by its tedium, people wouldn't go? I can't lie though – a Scout is to be trusted – it was glorious and beautiful and everyone should go there at least once.

Last Day – Home

I won't bore you with our return trip; it is ground we've already covered. It was also a straight run home with a final photo stop in Glen Coe and toilet break at the still expensive/still intimidating Green Welly Stop. We'd covered a lot of distance during the week. All in, we'd driven a little short of 940 miles and Explorers had walked 34 miles of the Great Glen Way. We'd spent just short of £700 on accommodation and close to £450 on food – all of which meant the trip had come in about £100 over budget, not bad really. We overspent by a fair margin on transport and accommodation (we promised we wouldn't but got lazy about camping); fortunately though, we underspent on food, so it all balanced out in the end.

I still say there is no such thing as a bad experience; it all depends on how you choose to deal with it. From the insanely creaky hostel above the chip shop in Thurso to the wind-blasted landscape of Altandhu, from the strange German dressed as a lime in the Broadford Health Centre Hostel on Skye, marking his territory with crisps and an oversized teapot, to the slick marketing of Scots' fiddle-dee-di along the Great Glen, this trip had already made an indelible mark in the minds of those who came along.

Thinking back, there was no way our decrepit old Land Rover Discoverys would have managed the journey, and fragile though our minibus seemed, it was a good ten years younger than either of our old 'Discos'. The bus had it's moments but it made it round the road without serious mishap, and being realistic, with the gear we ended up taking, we needed all the extra space it provided. We did have to explain several times to people that we weren't Scouts from Fife but by the middle of the week we stopped correcting people.

So what did we learn, or was that even the point? I think it's probably more apposite to ask what was re-affirmed, and I would say that was friendships. I think we could go almost anywhere as a group and enjoy ourselves, even the things that didn't go so well can be remembered with good humour. By the time our young folk get to the Explorer Section, most of them will have known each other for ten or more years. Since Scouts is entirely elective, those who don't get along so well tend to fade away – what is left is distilled friendship, concentrated good cheer and the kind of easy understanding that only comes from long acquaintance and among leaders it can be an even longer span of time. Would we do it if we didn't like each other? Of course not. Would we want to be around young people for whom we had no time? No.

There is a genuine mutual respect in our group, and while we may joke and poke fun, we all know where the line is and we don't cross it. It's not just about not being horrible to each other, it's about not taking offence. As a group our Explorers are endlessly affable, this is not to say they're soft, because they're not – they just don't take offence easily and are not overly prone to giving it. It really was a very happy coincidence they all found each other and joined our

Scout group – or perhaps it was no coincidence. Either way, I am grateful they did and I got to spend time with them.

Epilogue

This book took a while to write; for many reasons and sometimes none, it took longer than I expected. As I write this it's been almost three years since we returned from our northern odyssey but we still talk about it. Since then, we've walked the entirety of the Great Glen Way. The route has been modified to accommodate cyclists, the kind of tracks that suit narrow bicycle wheels (long straight cycle paths) but don't necessarily suit walkers. The canal sections of the route remain unchanged, but sections, specifically the old railway bed along the banks of Loch Oich, have been flattened and resurfaced. The sections of canal towpath between Banavie (Neptune's Ladder) and Gairlochy were always a bit tedious, but the balance was in the rest of the route: the Fairy Glen, now felled and gone, the bucolic old railway line along Loch Oich, now a cyclist's superhighway… We thought we might not return, but we probably will. The British Waterways campsites remain (we still have our toilet keys) and for novice walkers, it's still one of the best options in terms of access and flexibility, and the scenery remains as winsome as ever, which I think we still take for granted.

Unfortunately, the microcabins by Invermoriston on Loch Ness are no longer there – they traded them in for chalets. The cost to rent chalets is a good bit beyond that which we can budget for Scouts and to be honest, I don't think they'd appreciate the business. As it was, we received some thunderous looks from the motorhome crowd who were there on the same night – I mean, we weren't noisy, I think some people just expect to be miserable. It's all about balance though – as one door closes a window opens (or something). On a previous trip, while climbing down to the water's edge (the better to spy Nessie) I slipped on rocks and fell hard. That group, long since moved on to university and the working world, just laughed cruelly. Well, that might be an exaggeration, but they did derive more mirth than was reasonable from my misfortune. Since the microcabins are gone now, I won't fall over again, at least not there anyway. This is an affliction of advancing years – I'm not even that old, but I'm nowhere near as fleet as I used to be, so I have to be very careful where I put my feet lest I fall on my arse.

Interesting (and apparently hilarious) though that is, what I meant to say was, we found an excellent hostel near Invergarry called Saddle Mountain. I think we can all agree the title is more in keeping with the client base it serves, as opposed to Sandra's (for example) which sounds like a sauna which might offer extras. The hostel was clean, spacious and comfortable and not at all squeaky or redolent of chips, and the owners were great – in fact it was so good we stayed an extra night (that it was raining also figured in our decision). If you're walking the Great Glen Way or travelling in the area more generally, in the absence of the microcabins on Loch Ness, you should go there – it's really very nice.

Looking at photos of Explorers as they posed in front of points around the extreme north and west coasts of Scotland close to two years ago, they look a lot younger than they do now. They've filled out, they're no longer adolescents - they are young adults. Recently we had a belated Christmas party, we call it Festivus – it's something of a favourite on the Explorer Calendar. It's not an original idea, and you can search for details on the Internet. It is however, how should I put this, an interesting night? They might be 'Scouts' but they're like most other 16 years olds, and it's a chance to go a bit daft away from parental constraints. Lewis and I were sitting watching it all develop, and as one Explorer launched into a rendition of The Seekers' 'Georgie Girl' and several others fell off their chairs laughing so hard they couldn't breath, he leant over and said to me, 'Look at what you've created.'

In time they'll move on to university or some other new thing and leave us behind – and that is as it should be. But, if they do well, and I mean really well, us Leaders reserve the right to claim some of the credit. I mean, it's only fair, isn't it?

Extras

I was hoping participants of the trip would read this and add their own take in the form of speech bubbles throughout the book; however, revision for exams, after-school activities, 'internet research' and other assorted but unidentifiable activities took precedence. In place of that we have the following reviews. I'd liken them to DVD extras, but fear none of the young folk in this day and age of streaming knows what a DVD is.

Witty in places and harsh in others – Leader Number Three is off the Christmas card list – what follows is the unedited sum total of views in their own words from the young people who took this trip.

John-Andrew M, 14

I first joined the Explorer Scouts at the tender age of 13 years, 11 months and 14 days, and from that first fateful evening I knew it was for me. The thrill of adventure was positively coursing through my veins on our first outing to the village chippy. The conversations were suitably deranged and Paul's charisma (as you have probably gathered by now) was beyond compare. Thus you can imagine the boundless joy of being presented with the opportunity to spend an entire week with the Explorers, touring one of the finest landscapes on this earth: Luxembourg! (Just kidding we could never afford that.) Seriously though, Scotland is a wonderful place to see, but why am I prattling on about that when you've just read a whole book about it. The point of this bit (yes, it does have a point – I was surprised too) is to give you some idea of what the trip was like for us, and a different perspective from Paul's somewhat cynical descriptions. (Joking Paul, we love you really).

The walking part was received with mixed opinions from the group as a whole, but overall we all enjoyed it. We've all done the full Great Glen Way since and this was a good taster. I think the days were well enjoyed, especially after an entire hour melted away to my expert telling of 'the monk joke'. (If you are not familiar with this masterpiece of comedy then set aside at least 20 minutes and read it here: http://www.boyscouttrail.com/content/joke/youre_not_a_monk-605.asp. You might then understand why a cheeky grin and a wink was all that kept me from being placed – head first – in the adjacent canal!)

However, the nights weren't as good. Although the campsites were of pretty high quality, especially with keys to the ablutions, a combination of our frankly appalling shopping skills and the whole sleeping in a bag seemed to sour the mood a tad, but on the second night we watched the ISS pass overhead on it's 17,150 mph orbit of the Earth, which raised our spirits a bit, whilst Michael (Leader Number Three) took some soft focus pictures of the sky and loch for his instasnap tweetmatic grambook thingamajig, coining the new phrase '#toteslegitballs' to accompany them.

I would sum this section up with a quote about camping that Paul made a few years later, but unfortunately it has a rude word in it, and it would be simply awful if this became an audiobook and some young, impressionable children where to overhear the calm, seductive voice of Patrick Stewart saying a naughty word, so suffice to say, camping is one of those activities which appeals to a certain character trait that was thankfully under-represented in our group.

The road trip element was a whole different kettle of fish. Most of the days were spent quoting Monty Python, annoying Alastair (quite a fun pastime should the opportunity arise) and singing demonic-esque chants in C minor, arranged by our very own budding choirmaster, Ally. Most of the nights were spent in hostels rather than camping, which was a nice change. We mostly enjoyed the warmth, played cards and made good use of the better cooking facilities (those of us who knew how, that is).

I should probably stop around now as you all stopped reading halfway through paragraph one anyway. To round off I would thoroughly recommend a trip of this ilk to anyone who would listen (all six of you). However, heed this warning: alphabet soup is good, but two tins won't last 10 people three days!

Andrew C, 15

This was my very first trip away with the Longniddry Explorer group, but I knew the group fairly well and really enjoyed myself. Despite living in Scotland my entire life, there are many wonderful places that I have never visited, and this trip allowed me to visit a lot of them, as well as bringing up some good memories of places I had been to before.

There were also a few items I was able to tick off my bucket list, such as visiting John O'Groats. To be honest, not the most interesting place, but the sign that showed all the distances and directions of cities around the world really gave a sense of how large the world really is.

A good moment was when we arrived at Durness (I had been there before) and I remembered about Cocoa Mountain, which is a shop that makes possibly the greatest hot chocolate I have had in my life. When your cup is overflowing with cream, marshmallows and sprinkled with cocoa powder, you know that you've made a good decision.

The best part of the trip by far though, was when Paul had convinced us that we didn't have a place to stay for the night, and that we would likely be camping again, and then we turned into the hobbit cabin campsite on the edge of Loch Ness. I vividly remember the whole minibus cheering and whooping in celebration, with Paul and the other leaders laughing.

There was a beautiful sunset that evening, and it was a definite high point. Overall, I thoroughly enjoyed all aspects of the trip, from the banter in the minibus and laying out watching the stars on the west coast to Sandra's hostel in Thurso and Broadford Backpackers on the Isle of Skye. It was a great trip, and I would do it again in a heartbeat.

When I first joined Explorers it was more like two different groups: the new Scouts-Turned-Explorers and the older bunch including the leaders. We didn't chat with the other group the same way we would chat with each other. The October trip around Scotland, which was my first Explorer trip, seemed to me like the true start to Explorers as we learned that it was not like Scouts, where the leaders are more like teachers and Scouts the pupils, but more like one big happy family where everyone gets along with each other. At the start of the trip I felt like we were still having our own conversations within our groups and not including the leaders as much as we ought to but throughout the trip I really feel like we did start to come together as one group rather than two. I believe that I only became a proper member of the Longniddry Explorers after that trip – oh, and after the series of increasingly gruesome tasks and challenges that are the fabled Explorers' initiation ceremony.

The part of the trip that I enjoyed most – other than Ally's amazing singing – would probably be when we stayed in the microcabins just outside of Fort Augustus. Not only were they a welcome break from camping in tents (not many tents have heaters) but they also had a fantastic view over Loch Ness. We spent most of the evening in our microcabins playing different card games and talking.

I would like to finish by saying a big thank you to the person that made the trip possible – Paul. Not only does Paul give up two hours of his life every week to run Explorers but he also spends his free time planning and arranging these trips for us. If Explorers didn't exist then I would probably spend my Sunday nights doing drugs or homework, just kidding, I hate homework.

George S, 15

Why Paul thought that giving a group of 13 year old's a fair sum of money (about £50) and letting them loose in a supermarket to plan and buy their own meals for the first few nights would be a good idea, escapes me. Spaghetti hoops, hot dogs and super noodles are not the only food available to those who wish to be adventurous. After the first shopping trip I think we learned our lesson as to what you could actually make using only a camping stove. The trips to the shops after that were a little more successful as we bought real food and left out the cornflakes (so no ducks could be viciously assaulted and no crazy sandwiches could be made). As before there were some 'interesting' purchases but this time they were accompanied by real meals.

Having learned from this experience, the second time we walked the Great Glen Way, myself and the others were better prepared. Or so we thought. This time we did it in the summer and despite the improvement that good food and a decent sleep could provide, they did nothing to counteract the increase in midge population that seemed to be out to eat us all alive. Despite this, the experience I gained was essential for both my Duke of Edinburgh expeditions and for future Explorer trips where we could all sit and watch the freshly initiated explorers go through the same super-noodley struggle that we went through and laugh.

The trip itself was great fun. It felt like just a group of friends doing a tour of Scotland. A tour that included horrible hostels, poor pizza service and copious amounts of card games.

All jokes aside, a big thank you to Paul for making our group what it is, arranging all the wonderful trips and putting up with our shenanigans year after year as well as teaching us life lessons such as, 'Buy some actual food not god damn marshmallow fluff!' I highly recommend to you all to at least once in your life try the incredibly enjoyable experience that is touring Scotland by not fully planning your journey and staying only in hostels with a star rating of less than two.

Ally S, 15

Some of my favourite trips away have been with the Scouts. Unlike going on school trips, you're not bound by rules, of both the health and safety and the social kind. With Scouts, you aren't bound to try and fit in; you can be yourself, whether the others want you to or not. Indeed, the in-jokes and constant low-level ribbing makes the whole thing feel like a large, dysfunctional family (or maybe they just hate me – I honestly can't tell).

This trip didn't disappoint. I went home buzzing with new memories: some good, like travelling to Dunnet Head, the most northerly point in the British Isles, some fearful, such as visiting the eerie soft toy graveyard known as Fairy Glen, and some which I'm sure the others did not appreciate, such as trying my first energy drink just before a three-hour bus journey (in retrospect, not my best decision ever). One of the best experiences was staying a night in the barrels nicknamed Hobbits next to Loch Ness. In our room, affectionately titled Boromir, we spent the night in heated discussion of various topics, card games and laughing at one hilarious occurrence involving Harry's leg, a blanket, and much screaming (I think I'll leave the details of that one private, on second thoughts). Even the bus journeys were fun, involving singing more ABBA songs than I ever thought I would, and I'm sure everyone hoped I would. I think I got much closer to everyone else in the troop.

Overall, I loved the entire trip, and hope to be going on many more with the rest of my fellow Scouts soon.

I did my 500 words. I actually did 652. Are you happy now Paul? Am I your favourite now?

You'd be forgiven for thinking that Scotland is a rubbish holiday destination because it's cold, wet and dreary. But it's because it's cold, wet and dreary that it's a great holiday destination. I think it's best if I compare it to our Scout leader Paul Brown. If you want glamour, beauty and passion, you go to a supermodel. Kate Moss, for instance. But if it's something else you're after, something rugged, strong, but somehow charming, you go to Paul. Paul is very much the living embodiment of the Scottish Highlands, to Kate Moss' Cyprus.

But whereas Kate Moss is all out of ideas after the first few years of marriage, if you dive deep into Paul Brown you will discover that he has many treasures hidden within. (I should mention that at this point, I'm talking about Cyprus and Scotland, not Kate Moss and Paul Brown, even though I am further extending the metaphor. I recommend delving deep into Scotland, and not Paul Brown.) Some of my favourite treasures include:

A very picturesque bay, hidden away by steep rocky headlands that fall somewhere between a cliff and a hill. I can't quite remember where the bay is located – it might be near Smoo Cave. But if you do stumble across it then it is worth a visit. It has many caves, stacks and dunes, and has sand whiter than the 2016 Academy Awards

Ceremony. I also spotted a very dark cave ideal for hiding treasure/drugs/bodies, so if there are any smugglers reading, try setting up your base of operations there. Alternatively, if there are any police officers reading, consider this as a tip-off.

Another place I should touch upon is everybody's favourite hostel in Thurso: Sandra's Backpackers. A quick look at TripAdvisor will tell you that people visiting Thurso have been led to believe that the town has a line-up of hotels to rival that of Dubai or Monte Carlo. Either that or they can't read well enough to tell the difference between 'Hotel' and 'Hostel'. That is the only explanation for some of the reviews, which highlight things such as 'cheap jam' and 'grey towels'. Of the 74 reviews, 31% are 'Terrible.' Of that 74% of 'Terrible' reviews, 100% of them were written by people who were clearly expecting a hotel to rival the Savoy in London. These people were left disappointed. What Sandra's Backpackers isn't, is a five-star hotel in an exclusive location, with Sky Plus and a spectacular sea view. What Sandra's Backpackers is, is a cheap hostel with character. Reception doubles as a fish and chip shop, which, once you ignore the fire risk, is a brilliant idea. Inside, you will find a common room and kitchen area full of interesting bearded men and women in bobble hats and cardigans, full of amusing stories, usually involving sheep. There is a cupboard with an extensive VHS collection, and elsewhere in the building there is probably a working VHS player. In the rooms there are bunk beds which are comfortable enough, and there is a bathroom with a shower, toilet and sink.

That's it really, further evidence that it is not Buckingham Palace, but a hostel in North Scotland.

We all loved the atmosphere of Sandra's, and it has a special place in all our hearts. It has become a place of myth and legend back at the Scout hut, with plenty of stories about the hostel being told round the campfire. I would tell some of these stories, but we at Scouts have agreed that 'what happens in Sandra's stays in Sandra's' and must not leave under any circumstances, even if you are being interrogated by ISIS."

Besides, telling people all about Lewis' shower incident would be a dick move.

Harry R, 14

As I had been on many Scout trips in the past, when I got on the coach at the start of the trip, I assumed that I knew roughly what was in store. I was however – and for the better – completely wrong. There was far more freedom for one thing, and a sense of mutual respect between the leaders and Explorers that was completely unlike what we were used to. This did however come with the fact that there was far more freedom than there was on previous trips. This did come with a slight downside, as we were completely free to buy whatever rubbish we thought we would need to keep starvation, but not malnutrition, at bay (much to the dismay of Paul and, when teatime came around, ourselves as well). Luckily we were relatively fast learners, and bought proper food before the number of rice crispy squares purchased made the van collapse under its own weight.

However, one of the more interesting and slightly terrifying developments occurred in the Hobbit cabins, in which it became a trend for a certain individual to turn off the lights and declare that it was 'special time', and by the time you had managed to turn the lights back on, you realise that where you were sitting, there was another person who had been slammed against the wall roughly a centimetre to the right of where your head had been, with a hand so large some say it could block out the sun, leaving you wondering if you would be able to survive the night.

Despite this, the week was a great success! From the beautiful landscape of the highlands, to the invention of the infamous cornflake and brown sauce sandwich (which I would highly recommend to anyone, and defend from critics with my life) to even the day-long caffeine induced Sweeny Todd rehearsals. It was a great experience, and I look forward to any and all future trips with the Explorers.

Leader Number Three, 19

Going on a trip away with Paul is an experience to say the least. I have had the pleasure of going on many week-long and countless weekend trips with him over the years, so this was not my first rodeo. As you are well aware (because you've got this far into the book) Paul appointed himself leader and Commander-in-chief of the trip, but as with all leaders it was really those in the background who did all the work. This role fell to Lewis and myself (Leaders Number Two and Three, respectively). Whether it was cooking, cleaning out the minibus or getting Paul into his sedan chair then helping some of the smaller children lift it, Lewis and I were at his beck and call. The small ornate bell that he used to summon us suspiciously went missing somewhere between Inverness and Thurso.

The trip itself started off with all the same anticipation and excitement that we can only guess the great explorers felt in their day. The checking of gear, the questioning of whether or not something is really necessary, the packing of a harpoon gun just to be safe and the ripping of children out of the claw-like clutches of their parents. There is a certain level of pressure you are put under when looking after someone else's children for a week that isn't helped when you discover what they've bought for their food for the first few days – there were probably just a handful of calories to go round the lot of them. This, they would not get from their parents. I was glad they started to eat properly as the week drew on because I don't know if I could have handled the judgemental looks from their families as we handed back their beloved children, mere skeletons of what they were when they were handed into our care. But it's all character building, a life lesson, and something we'll all build on in the future.

I feel that there has been a failure to mention the almost constant berating I got from Paul and Lewis purely down to me being young and further away from death than them. For some reason it was a bad thing that I understood some of the pop culture references the 'whippersnappers' were talking about. It all came to a head when Paul tried his hardest to barge his way into the conversation with an ill-timed Gerry and the Pacemakers reference that went so far over their heads it almost dented the minibus roof. We also had to stop for a short break in a day's travelling to allow Paul to come to terms with Top of the Pops no longer being broadcasted on the 'televisual set'.

Every once in a while, in the mornings after we had been camping, you might catch a glimpse of Paul exiting his hike tent. It truly is something to behold. The performance starts well before the tent is even opened. The tent will start to gently sway, slowly picking up pace, the guy ropes straining with the to and fro as Paul frantically tries to get dressed within, then the doorway will slowly start to unzip purely down to the pressure that the flysheet is under. After the warning grunts and moans to alert all who are around to clear the landing strip, Paul starts to emerge. What happens next takes only a matter of seconds and is over as quickly as it had begun. With a roll and pike that is usually only kept for Olympic divers, Paul escapes his nylon tomb of the previous night. This occurs with all the beauty of childbirth (similar levels of blood, mucus and what have you) and the grace of a crème caramel being dropped from a great height. It finishes with Paul, panting heavily like a sick dog, sprawled out on the grass, the morning dew mixing with his tears and his tent now long collapsed lying behind him. None of us ever really know if it's all part of the act that he manages to dismount and dismantle his tent with one fell swoop, or whether Paul is just a key structural part for his tent. We didn't have the heart to ask.

It may well be the fact that just the act of getting up in the morning is so demanding, both physically and mentally, on Paul, that you don't want to cross him until at least the afternoon. I remember fondly one morning Paul giving a (some would say 'passionate', others 'aggressive') lecture to the gathered masses on how to roll a sleeping mat correctly and how this would free up, from what I could see, no space in the minibus whatsoever. But that's just what he's like, and as each morning turned into afternoon Paul would return to his usual self. The young people on the other hand, I don't think have ever unrolled their mats since out of fear that they could not live up Paul's exacting standards. Many of them still have visible tics when kit lists are handed out and they see that they have to bring something to sleep on.

Sleeping with Paul (steady, same room different beds) can only be described as a race. Whoever falls asleep first will get the better night's sleep. Saying that, Paul will have a good night's sleep either way (never trust what that man says). If you are lucky enough and have snuck away in time to get into bed and drift off to sleep before he has even thought of slipping into his sleeping bag, you'll be in the clear. But, if the hostel's mattress is not up to the five star standards you are used to and you're kept up, you're fresh out of luck! First, you'll think you're experiencing a small to moderate earthquake. The walls will shake, tiles will clatter to the ground outside and the glass of water on your bedside will tremble ominously. But soon you'll start to wonder if you are in fact sleeping in the middle of a walrus breeding ground and will half expect the already trembling walls to be broken down by a swarm of titillated walri.

You hastily reach for your harpoon gun (glad to have brought it), finger hovering over the trigger, waiting for the last thing you see to be a pair of tusks lurching out of the darkness toward you. But no! All you are met by is Paul sleeping like a very loud, hairy baby. For most, a night indoors is a welcome relief from the cold hard rocky ground of the camping experience, but not for Lewis and me. The cold embrace of the rocky ground was what we dreamed of (well, what we would have dreamed of if we got any sleep) whilst we were frantically hanging on to our bedframes to avoid being inhaled by Paul. Soon, however, we too fell asleep, the exhaustion of the day taking over.

It's something that they don't tell you when you first start to look after other people's children: it's tiring. A constant worry of whether or not what you are doing is even remotely interesting to the screen-addicted, energy drink drinking youth of today is a real issue, let alone having to make sure they are eating correctly. How do their parents do it? So every night would roll round and you'd all just fall into bed only to wake up fresh for the next exciting day.

I remember the day when we packed the minibus for the last time and all found our usual seats and set off. There was a definite feeling of relief, mainly due to the fact that everyone had survived, got on (as well as could be expected) and had enjoyed themselves. At least that's the impression I got from the young people. From my point of view it was a great time, a chance to see more of the country that I lived in, a chance to escape the demanding highflying lifestyle that I lead, but most of all, a chance to get to know the people I was with better. Be it the younger or the older, I feel I gained a better understanding of everyone who was there. A chance to share ideas, opinions, jokes and also time. It's the time – no matter where you go, it's the time investment that you all agree to spend together away from everything. They really were a great group of people and it's that type of group that makes you walk into your quiet house after the trip and miss it. You miss the new vistas that greet you when you turn the next corner, the interesting people who you meet along the way, and the people you just spent a week in a smelly minibus with that could have broken down at any moment. It was that feeling we all knew we were soon going to feel as we turned back onto the road that we had come north on, but this time going south. (Really, I couldn't wait for a hot meal, warm bath and a night in my own bed away from all of them! But that doesn't have the same ring to it.)

Many thanks for reading, I'd be grateful if you could leave a review on Amazon – I don't mind if it's a bad one, as long as it's humorous.

Other titles I've written, (if this one hasn't totally put you off) are available.

On Arran – A short travelogue about the island.

The Great Glen Way – An account of a previous group's stumblings along the long distance walk of the same name.

Search for them on Amazon.

The innocent Scottish icon before our ill-advised, alcohol inspired pincer movement.

Printed in Great Britain
by Amazon